EARTH ROADS

A Practical Guide to
Earth Road Construction and Maintenance

JACK HINDSON

EARTH ROADS

A Practical Guide to
Earth Road Construction and Maintenance

Edited and revised by
John Howe and Gordon Hathway
of Intermediate Technology Transport Ltd.

I T PUBLICATIONS

Published by Intermediate Technology Publications Ltd,
103–105 Southampton Row, London WC1B 4HH, UK.

ISBN 0 903031 84 1

Typeset by Inforum Ltd, Portsmouth
Printed in Great Britain by SRP, Exeter

Contents

Editors' Foreword

One of the most glaring differences between the developed and developing countries is in the densities of their respective road networks. Indeed the density or quality of a country's road system is often used as a measure of its state of development. That roads are an essential ingredient of the development process is indisputable, but it is generally believed that the limited resources of most developing countries and the cost of modern road construction has prevented rapid expansion or improvement of their systems.

Yet in the early stages of development it is doubtful if modern high-cost roads are necessary: there is abundant evidence to show that the existence of a means of communication is more important than its quality. There is, in fact, a very considerable literature on 'low-cost' road construction and there have been many conferences around the world devoted solely to the subject. However, it is arguable whether the roads thus described are truly low-cost. Most of the descriptions given of construction methods presume the knowledge and skills of a graduate civil engineer and the use of complex equipment.

The result is a technology largely incomprehensible to the layman, and a road that is not low-cost. One of the author's intentions in this book is to fill the need for a simplified description of road planning and construction at the most elementary level.

However, the author's prime purpose is much more radical. It is to explain how *earth* roads could be constructed and maintained in a way that would prevent their progressive and often rapid destruction by erosion due to the uncontrolled flow of water. The emphasis throughout is on the proper control of water reaching the road, and on basic principles of soil conservation – it is this aspect which makes the book unique. The approach is that of a soil conservationist to the building of an earth structure: a simple road. The focus is quite deliberately on roads designed to carry a few dozen vehicles a day at most. Fully engineered gravel or bitumen surfaced roads are not considered.

The text covers two different basic designs of earth road called, for convenience, 'village' and 'market' roads. These are not precisely defined operationally, but the essential difference is the level of usage, from a few vehicles per day or week (village) to perhaps fifty vehicles per day (market).

Some of the descriptions given are unorthodox, particularly the use of diversion banks, which are a major means of controlling erosion but, as the author explains, the orthodox approach to road construction produces either a very expensive structure that can be built only by skilled engineers, or one that rapidly deteriorates to uselessness. The methods described in this book deserve respect because they are not based on untried theories, but are the direct result of building and maintaining earth roads for a period of more than twenty years in the northernmost parts of Zambia. They are based on the accumulated experience of extensive trial and error, and, despite their apparent simplicity, they can be seen to derive from sound scientific principles.

Emphasis is placed on the achievement of low construction costs by adopting a low-speed natural alignment for the road, using local labour-intensive building methods where possible, and minimizing the cost of earth-moving by use of material along the line of the road. The use of gravel, wheelbarrows to haul earth and borrow-pits as a source of material are not recommended except to meet extreme local conditions.

The use of diversion banks, drifts and splashes also has the effect of positively controlling the speed of vehicles. This is arguably more effective than the conventional 'design speed' approach, which does not prevent those vehicles capable of travelling fast from doing so, and thus damaging the road. The resultant reduction in road damage is an essential part of the success of these methods.

Implicit in the author's approach to low-cost earth road construction is the recognition that, in addition to conventional motorized transport, such roads may be used by a range of much simpler vehicles including wheelbarrows and handcarts, animal-drawn carts and pedal-driven devices. These simple vehicles can meet many rural transport needs and are often more appropriate to the financial resources of the rural population than motorized vehicles.

The task of the editors has been simply to update some of the figures and generalize the colloquial terms in the original manuscript. Also, to achieve a publication that could be afforded by many of its intended readers it has been necessary somewhat to shorten and reorganize the text, though this has not resulted in the omission of any important material.

The text is divided into four major parts. The first deals with the drainage principles and techniques which form the basis of the road design and construction methods proposed. Part two covers the planning of the road, with the emphasis on route selection, surveying and marking. The third section describes construction methods, and the final part deals with the subsequent maintenance operations. Appendix 1 describes the operation and use of some simple pieces of surveying equipment referred to in the main text. To assist the reader a glossary of road construction terms is included as Appendix 2.

Metric units are used throughout. For the most part the S.I. system has been adopted but in certain cases the centimetre (cm) has been used to facilitate understanding by likely users of the book.

CHAPTER 1
Introduction

1. Erosion on Earth Roads

Erosion is the wearing away of soil by water and, usually to a much lesser extent, by wind. It varies enormously from one country to another and even from one district to another. In some areas there is no erosion at all but in the majority of cases erosion is likely to be a major problem, causing considerable damage to agriculture and to roads.

The most usual cause of erosion is rain. Instead of the rain falling gently during many months of the year it is concentrated into only a few months. During these wet months much of the rain comes in short, sharp storms which may be very intense. These very heavy storms are the major cause of erosion and are responsible for the widespread damage which so often occurs on earth roads.

Erosion on the carriageway (where the traffic runs) or in the side drain of the road results from too much water being allowed to accumulate there. Most roads have a slight gradient (that is, they run uphill or downhill slightly) so, if much water does collect on them, it will begin to flow. As the volume of water increases so does its speed, causing the amount of erosion to increase to a much greater extent. This can be prevented by diverting all the water into the bush at intervals so that no excessive build-up of water is allowed to occur.

Figure 1(a) shows, in cross-section, a typical earth road that is being eroded along the carriageway, as a result of too much storm water being allowed to flow along the wheel tracks. Figure 1(b) shows another earth road which is also being severely eroded, this time in the side drains. This is because these drains have to take far too great a flow of storm water.

Obviously these roads will have only a short life if nothing is done to divert the flow of water. After a few years they will have eroded so much that they will not be worth repairing and new ones will have to be made.

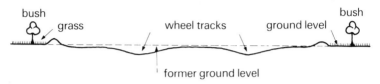

Figure 1(a). Erosion in wheel tracks.

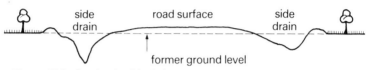

Figure 1(b). Erosion in side drains.

Particular attention will be paid throughout the book to the problem of erosion. The intention is to explain how damage can be prevented by the adoption of certain simple soil conservation practices. *The aim throughout is the efficient control and disposal of run-off water.*

2. Soil Conservation Principles and Road Drainage

The problem is to provide a permanent earth road which is designed to serve present and future requirements. It must be done as cheaply as possible; therefore every operation must be fully justified.

Any earth road will fail, sooner or later, if *avoidable erosion* due to water flow is allowed to continue unabated. Each season the level of the road will sink a little due to removal of soil; the more it sinks the more difficult it will be to drain the water off the road. This means that erosion damage although imperceptible at first, is liable to increase rapidly in later years. Avoidable erosion due to lack of water control may easily be prevented, as will be described in this book.

However, earth roads are also subject to *unavoidable erosion*. This is the loss of soil from the road surface, either in the form of dust which has been pulverized by the passing of traffic, or as mud splashed out of the tracks by passing vehicles during heavy rain. These losses are difficult to prevent, but are nearly always insignificant compared with the loss of soil by avoidable erosion. They can also be easily replaced by using simple maintenance procedures (see Chapter 10).

Solutions to the problems of avoidable earth road erosion can be obtained by the application of the general principles of soil conservation, particularly as they are applied by farmers. For example, various gradients may be used to make water flow through arable land. However, in practice a gradient steeper than 1 in 250[1] is never used in ordinary soils for fear of causing erosion in the bed of the furrow during a storm. Where water does have to flow, it is run out on to permanent grass where it finds its way straight down the hill, at a gradient often far steeper than 1 in 250. Normally no erosion will occur in this grassed disposal area if the grass is preserved and not destroyed by cultivation or overgrazing and if the volume of water discharged during a heavy storm is not excessive.

Some disposal areas may have to be excavated and levelled off to the required shape, and perhaps grassed over too, before the run-out water can be turned on to them. (Grass will grow naturally on nearly all topsoils within a year or two if left undisturbed. This grass growth is not shown in most of the figures, in order to improve clarity.)

There are three shapes of waterway suitable for this type of work. (Figures 2(a), (b) and (c)). In practice there is little difference between these three cross-sections. In each of them the flow is spread out over a wide area in the form of a thin sheet of water. This moves only slowly through the mat of grass foliage, so the grass has a good chance to grow. This is the method that is used to conduct storm water straight down earth slopes steeper than 1 in 250. Compare the above waterways with a deep, steep-sided drain (Figure 3) carrying the same flow of water down the same slope. Here the water will flow much deeper, and hence much faster, because it cannot spread out in a shallow layer over a wide area. The grass will be unable to survive in this drain, and soil erosion will soon set in, starting a gully. This type of drain would be safe only on very flat land where the water stands or flows very slowly. When an experienced conservationist has to make provision for water to discharge straight down a hill he looks for, or excavates, wide shallow waterways like those in Figure 2; the wider the better. He would never

---

[1]See Appendix 1 for an explanation of this term.

(a). *Flat — correct.*

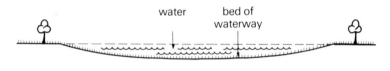

(b). *Dished — correct.*

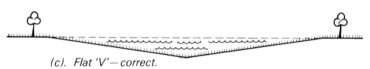

(c). *Flat 'V' — correct.*

Figure 2. Wide, shallow waterways.

contemplate a cross-section like that of the deep narrow drain shown in Figure 3 because it would not grass over.

All these basic conservation principles apply also in the control and disposal of run-off water on earth road systems.

The earth roads that we are concerned with can be divided into two separate types, each with its own distinct method of construction and maintenance, which will be described in detail later. One of these types will be called a 'village' road and the other a 'market' road.

3. Village Roads — the 'Flat' Method
A village road is the simplest, cheapest road or track; it may run from one small village to another or to a farm, a small settlement, a

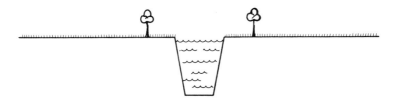

Figure 3. Deep, narrow drain—incorrect.

school or a dispensary. It may even run from one field to another on a farm for use, for example, by animal-drawn carts. All these village roads should be made flat with no side drain and no camber. On these village roads only one pair of wheel tracks will be formed by the passage of traffic; if these deepen they should be filled in. Any surface run-off water moving down the slope through the bush will be able to pass across the road at any point, just as if there were no road there at all. Erosion is adequately controlled by making diversion banks (see Chapter 2) where required along all village roads. Diversion banks are gentle humps across the road which divert all water into the surrounding bush. These banks will, of course, slow down motorized traffic, but the most important requirement on a village road, both in hilly and in flat country, is for slow, steady speeds in any weather and at any season of the year. Diversion banks help to ensure this. The carriageway itself is merely cleared of small bushes and trees including their roots (a process which will be referred to subsequently as stumping) and levelled so that water can pass across it in any direction.

Crossings
In Figure 4 the small watercourses A, B, C and D show how water might trickle across such a road when it rains. On the left of the diagram a larger watercourse, or stream, S, crosses over the road.

As the crossings A, B, C and D would be wet only when it rains, and as there is only infrequent traffic on a village road, there would be no trouble from mud at these crossings, particularly if the road were grassed. If, however, mud did form in one of the tracks where the water crosses, the addition of a few stones or a load or two of gravel would put it right. Often, throwing on more soil to fill in any depression is sufficient.

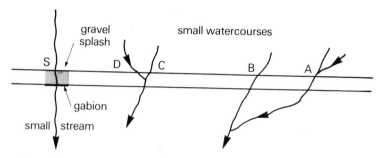

Figure 4. Water crossing a village road.

On the left of the diagram the stream S would definitely need attention. A lot more stones, etc. would have to be spread on the bed of this crossing. Storm water might tend to wash this away, in which case it would have to be stabilized by laying a length of rock-filled gabion (see Appendix 2) along the lower side as shown. (This subject is dealt with fully in Chapter 4.)

4. Market Roads — the 'High-Level' Method

Market roads carry more traffic than village roads. This type of road would run to a market, a food-buying depot, a rural development scheme or other important rural centre where traffic might amount to ten or twenty vehicles a day. In the dry season heavy lorries might use the road.

On the flat stretches of a market road, where the slope is less than 1 in 250, a bare earth drain (as in Figure 3) could be depended on not to erode, but as soon as the gradient of the road steepens to, say, 1 in 150 or steeper, then the flow must pass through grass and not over bare earth; this means that a wide flat drain becomes necessary. This method should therefore be adopted whatever the gradient.

The High-Level Method of Construction

Since they carry more vehicles than village roads, market roads must be cambered to allow water to run off into side drains. To achieve this the high-level method of construction should be used. The reasons for this are illustrated by means of Figures 5 (a), (b) and (c). In each of these examples the carriageway is 30cm above the

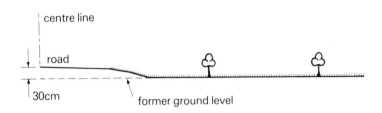

(a). Road built above ground level — incorrect.

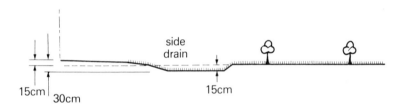

(b). The high-level method — correct.

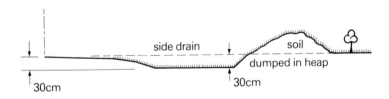

(c). Road built at ground level — incorrect.

Figure 5. Market road construction methods.

level of any shallow water which may be standing alongside the road, i.e. in the side drains in Figure 5 (b) and (c), and on the ground in Figure 5 (a). This 30cm 'freeboard' is necessary to enable the road to dry out a few centimetres below the surface. The land is flat in each case.

Figure 5(a) shows a road built completely above ground level by importing soil from a borrow site. This would be very expensive because of the cost of transporting the soil.

Figure 5(b) shows the high-level method. Soil for the road is dug and thrown from the side drain until the camber is high enough. A drain 15cm deep (the depth of one hoe-cut, approximately) and a compacted road 15cm high would give the required 30cm free-board. Since the drain and the camber are formed in one operation the cost of construction is minimized.

Figure 5(c) shows what would happen if the road were built at ground level. Soil has to be excavated to form the camber and side drains and dumped uselessly in the bush. Because the side drains are well below ground level, it is difficult or impossible to run water from them into the bush.

5. Village and Market Roads: Further Considerations

A market road will be drier than a village road because rain falling on the carriageway of the high-level road will, in theory, be shed off the sloping camber into the side drains. On a flat village road, on the other hand, there will be a tendency for rain water to stand in puddles instead of running off.

Again, the carriageway of a high-level road is about 30cm above the level of the bed of its side drains, so the soil in the road will tend to drain dry nearly down to the level of the bed of these drains. The carriageway will therefore remain a lot drier than it would do in the case of a flat village road which has no side drains at all.

Infrequent light traffic will do little damage to wet spots on a village road but, if traffic increases, these wet spots will soon turn into mud; if the wet weather continues, the road may become impassable.

Gravelling the surface reduces the risk of mud but transporting gravel is very expensive; instead it is far cheaper (and more satisfactory) to reduce the risk by raising the level of the road and cambering it, i.e. to make a high-level market road in place of a flat village road. Up to a point the higher it is raised (widening it at the same time to keep a good camber) the drier it will be. If mud still tends to form in places, due to the clay soil, then gravelling may have to be resorted to.

A market road will serve the needs of a district until it develops and the earth road begins to break up under the increased traffic. It will then have to be properly gravelled, perhaps throughout its length; reconstruction may even be necessary. *These are expensive operations involving expert knowledge and are not dealt with in this book.* Village and market roads are the two types which will be considered in this book. It is clear that the key to earth road performance is the proper control of water flow. The following chapters will show how this can be done.

PART 1

Water Control and Drainage Methods

CHAPTER 2
Diversion Banks

Diversion banks are fundamental to the proper performance of village roads. Also, many of the principles upon which they are based apply to the drainage of cambered market roads and to the siting of lead-off drains (see Chapter 3).

One sometimes sees a bush road which goes over the remains of an old anthill or passes near the foot of one. This is shown in Figure 6. The road to the left, and upstream, of the anthill may be eroding severely due to excessive storm water being trapped in it. When this flow meets the anthill it is unable to pass over it so the water has to force its way through the grass on the lower side of the road. Depending on the slope of the ground this flow of water may, or may not, return to the road further on. In Figure 6 the natural slope would take the water slightly away from the road. The section of road immediately below the anthill will therefore be completely

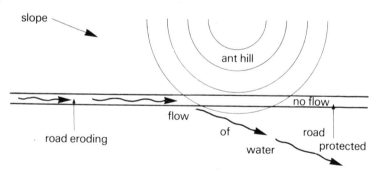

Figure 6. A natural diversion bank.

protected from any erosion due to run-off down the road. The water may tend to form ponds where the flow meets the rise of the anthill and mud may form at that point, but this is a very minor consideration compared with the fact that all flow has been diverted off the road. The presence of these long bumps in the road, which forces all the water off the road, affords an important, though localized, measure of protection from erosion.

Diversion banks are identical, in principle, to these natural ant-hills which divert the water, the only difference being that the former are made artifically, as and where required.

1. Practical Considerations

The bank forms a block in the road which diverts the water but allows the traffic to pass easily and safely, so long as it is not travelling at excessive speed. Associated with the diversion bank is a diversion drain which feeds the water into the bush. Soil for the bank is dug out of the diversion drain and thrown onto the road (Figure 7).

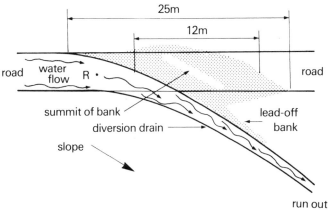

Figure 7. Diversion bank and drain.

Distance Between Diversion Banks
This can vary enormously. If storm water flows only very slowly onto the road from adjacent land, the diversions might be as much as 250m apart where the ground is flat. However, in steep country where a lot of run-off water reaches the road, they could in exceptional cases be as little as 30m apart.

Natural Diversions
There will be many of these along most road lines. Some will resemble diversion banks, e.g. anthills and other bumps. Other diversions are streams and minor watercourses due to undulating ground.

Figure 8 shows a road crossing two streams, A and B, a kilometre apart; there is a general slope down to the right. The ground rises a little in the middle, making it impossible for any of the flood in Stream A to pass on down the road into stream B. In other words, the rise in the road (that is, the watershed) forms an efficient natural diversion bank a kilometre long and perhaps 15m high.

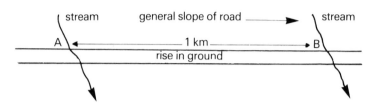

Figure 8.   A natural diversion bank.

In escarpment country a road running along a hillside will cross frequent gullies, etc. Each deep watercourse will divert the full flow (as in Figure 8) and no flow can pass on along the road and cause erosion, as it can in flat country where effective natural diversion points (e.g. streams, gullies, etc.) are few and far between.

Siting of Diversion Banks
Consider the example shown in Figure 9. It shows a village road crossing one stream and two small watercourses. All three can be relied on to divert a high flood without letting any water pass on along the road. Diversion banks are sited at D1, D2 and D3. These sites are chosen because the two long slopes appear likely to erode

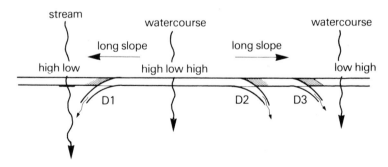

Figure 9.   Siting of diversion banks.

whereas the other four slopes do not. One diversion bank should suffice on the D1 slope, but two banks are considered necessary on the longer slope D2-D3.

If a concentrated flow of water reaches the road, as in a gully, from the bush on the upper side, try to take the flow straight across the road, as in Figure 10(a), instead of letting it run down the road to the next diversion point, as shown in Figure 10(b).

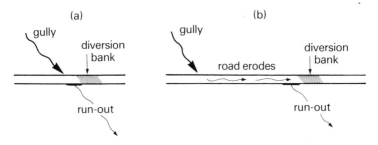

Figure 10. Gully crossing road.   (a). Correct.   (b). Incorrect.

There must always be some fall on the bed of the diversion drain so that it conducts the water away. For a short drain 5m long there should be a fall of at least 8cm (about 1 in 60 slope); a long drain should drop at least 8cm every 10m (1 in 125) although a steeper slope is preferable. Where possible a site should be chosen where the water can get away easily so that only a little work is required to complete the diversion drain and bank. Inevitably some sites are more difficult and a long drain and a big bank may be necessary. The slope of the drain must be continued across the road (i.e. near point R in Figure 7) so that the water flows to the diversion drain and does not stand on the road.

In flat country try to site diversion banks just above any slight drops (slopes) in the road as the necessary 8-16cm fall for the diversion drain will be found in only a few metres.

By diverting the flow off the road, the diversion bank protects the length of road below it. There is no point in making a diversion bank right at the bottom of a slope since there is no road there for it to protect. A big, strong diversion bank may be necessary, however, to protect a bridge or a drift if the road above is eroding badly.

There should always be a diversion bank immediately above a cutting (this is where a road has to be cut down some feet into the soil, as at the approach to a stream crossing where the stream bank is high and steep). This prevents any water running into the cutting from the road above it (Figure 11).

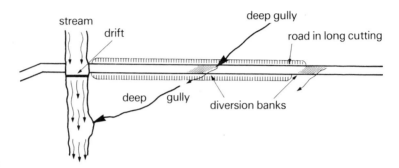

Figure 11. Diversion banks in cuttings.

Erosion in long cuttings can be troublesome because it is normally impossible to divert the flow out of the cutting. In some cases this may be overcome if, in the first instance, the road is sited to cross a gully halfway down the cutting, as shown in Figure 11. A diversion bank may then be made, discharging into the gully.

Often a natural undulation may be nearly big enough to make an efficient diversion bank (Figure 12). A little inexpensive topping up of the bank is all that is required. Diversion banks should be sited like this when feasible.

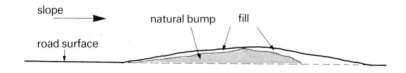

Figure 12. Diversion bank made from natural bump.

There may be occasions on a village road where there is excessive surface run-off water from the bush which would cause prolonged wetting of a long stretch of road. In such a situation the construction of a catchwater drain (see Chapter 5, Section 2) is merited, as in Figure 13. Allow for this drain and choose the site for the bank accordingly.

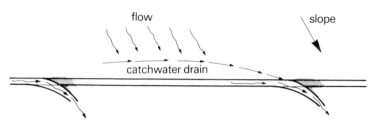

Figure 13. Catchwater drain diverting excessive run-off water.

Rocks are frequently found on hilly village roads. Labour can often be saved if the diversion bank can be sited to cover the rock. If, instead, the drain comes where the rock is, this will have to be dug out or broken down.

Reducing Erosion by Reducing Amount of Water

If storm water is diverted off the road at sufficiently close intervals there will be no erosion, and if there is a suitable place where the water can be diverted easily it should be done. The aim must be to prevent any dangerous build-up of storm water.

If the flow is well controlled, then a steep gradient on the diversion drains does not matter; they can be sited to discharge straight down the slope (Figure 7) or in whichever direction it is most convenient for the water to get away.

Paths Bringing Storm Water onto the Road

A very good way of reducing the amount of water on the road is to reduce the amount of storm water reaching it from the bush above.

Much of this water arrives down footpaths, cattle and cart-tracks etc., coming from the land above the road. If small diversion banks are made along all these tracks, the water is diverted into the bush and hardly any will reach the road; what does reach the road will arrive there long after the storm has passed. In some cases it may be worth starting the top diversion bank 400m or more from the road and inserting a number of banks below it, as in Figure 14.

It is a waste of time trying to divert water off a path if the path is sited along the bed of a slight valley, i.e. along the watercourse itself. (The same is true of any road.) If water is diverted off the path into the bush it will find its way back again onto the path because that is its natural watercourse.

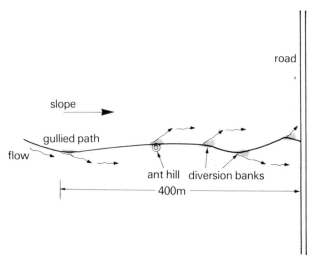

Figure 14. Diversion banks on footpaths.

In such cases the path (or road) should be re-sited to the side, up the hill a little above flood level, so that cross-drainage will then be possible. Always allow water to follow its natural watercourse wherever this is feasible.

2. Shape of Diversion Banks
Compared with diversion banks in flat country, those on hills have to be shorter and sharper, as explained below.

Diversion Banks on the Flat
Typical measurements for one of the larger banks are shown in Figure 15(a). The overall length of the bank is about 25m along the road (see Figure 7). Measured along the centre line of the road, the bank itself is about 12m long. The height to the top of the bank is 30cm (i.e. there is 30cm freeboard). The road therefore slopes up at 1 in 20, then down again at 1 in 20 as it goes over the bank. This bank could probably be taken at 40 km/h in a car, without inconvenience. The overall length of a diversion bank might be as short as 15m. Since the height of 30cm must be maintained such a bank would have a steeper gradient and would have to be traversed at a slower speed, say 25 km/h.

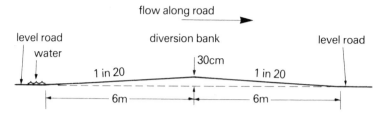

*Figure 15(a). Dimensions of diversion bank —
cross-section along road centre-line.*

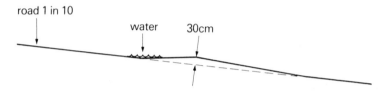

Figure 15(b). Incorrect bank on slope.

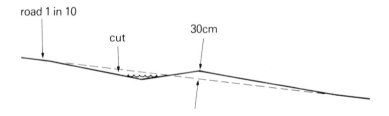

Figure 15(c). Correct bank on slope.

Diversion Banks On Hills

Two shapes of bank are shown in Figures 15(b) and (c). In the former case the shape is the same as on a flat road, but because it is built on a gradient, the slope of the upper bank is gentle. Therefore the water may begin to flow over the top, even if it is a big earthwork, and it will soon be washed away. The correct shape is shown in Figure 15(c). The upper slope of the bank is steeper and this can be relied upon to divert the water, but will obviously mean slower speeds for traffic. Remember that the slope on the downhill side of a diversion bank is steeper than the road itself, e.g. in Figure 15(c) the slope of the road is 1 in 10 but the slopes on the diversion bank and on the excavated drain, if any, are steeper, nearly 1 in 6. This makes it particularly important to avoid too steep a gradient along any section of the road.

Freeboard

As shown in Figure 15(c), the water channel is excavated a little so that the necessary freeboard (about 30cm) may be obtained without making too big (i.e. too expensive) a bank. This can be done on hills because it is easy to find run-outs, but in flat country it may be difficult to find any run-out at all if the water channel is deepened.

In flat country, therefore, all the freeboard must be obtained by raising the bank (about 30cm) and not by deepening the water channel at all. The principle must be that of a diversion bank rather than of a diversion drain.

In effect the bank dams the water flowing along the road and diverts it down the diversion drain.

CHAPTER 3
Lead-Off Drains

As the name implies, a lead-off drain is one that leads, or diverts, water from the side drain of a road on to the surrounding land for dispersal. Some people may think that it is sufficient if the water is removed from the side drain only when a minor watercourse is reached. This would be all right if these points occured at sufficiently close intervals, but this seldom happens. Generally the natural drainage lines are much too far apart and this makes artificial lead-offs, etc. essential. Lead-off drains are therefore used on market roads, to prevent too great a build-up of water in the side drain.

It is important to have efficient lead-off drains wherever they are required. One is shown, in plan, in Figure 16. The bolster blocks the side drain and diverts the flow down the lead-off drain. If the lead-off drain is to work efficiently it must have a gradient of about 1 in 125, or steeper, with a clear run-out at the end. The soil excavated from the lead-off drain should be moved towards the road to form the bolster.

1. Shape of Lead-Off Bolster
In Figure 16, the broken line outlines roughly the base of the bolster. The base widens where it crosses the side drain; it may be nearly 6m wide at that point so it will be quite a sizeable earthwork. The top of the lead-off bank and the top of the lead-off bolster should be at the same level throughout, as far as the end point P where it ties in to the road.

Every lead-off bolster should be fully stable and permanent. Cattle treading on it should not harm it much and, if a mistake has been made and a little storm water does flow over the top, it should do little damage. This is illustrated in Figures 17(a), (b) and (c). In each case the flood level of the water in the lead-off drain is indicated. Both (a) and (b) are stable but (c) is very unstable because of the short, steep slopes used in its construction.

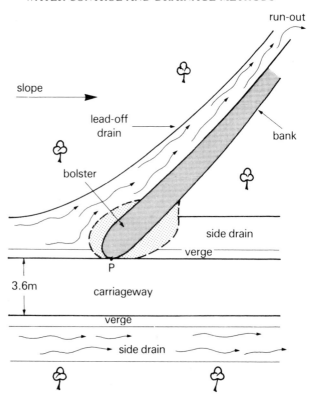

Figure 16. Plan of lead-off drain.

2. Choosing the Layout for Lead-Off Drains

Each lead-off bolster blocks the side drain at an angle of about 30 degrees, much the same as a diversion bank blocking a village road. In order to get the water well away from the road the lead-off drains are extended at a gradient of 1 in 125 for a sufficient distance to prevent the run-out flow reaching the road again. In Figure 18(a) there is no crossfall on the road so the lead-off drains are the same both sides. In Figure 18(b), where there is a crossfall, lead-offs from the upper side are longer and more expensive than in (a). This is necessary so that the run-off water from the upper lead-off drain, which will tend to run back towards the road, is caught in the next lead-off drain, rather than in the side drain. Lead-offs from the

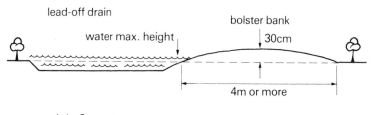

(a). Correct.

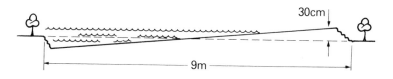

(b). Correct

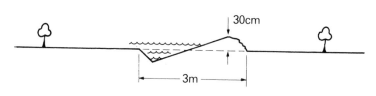

(c). Incorrect.

Figure 17. Lead-off drains in flood.

lower side are very short and inexpensive so more are inserted. This is why the side drain can be reduced in size, as shown.

Note that village road diversion banks always discharge to the lower side whereas lead-off drains on market roads sometimes discharge to the upper side (Figure 18(b)).

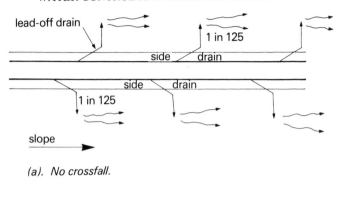

(a). No crossfall.

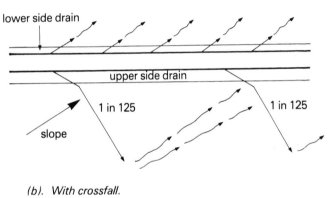

(b). With crossfall.

Figure 18. Layout of lead-off drains.

3. 'T' Lead-Off Drains

Normally lead-off drains are at an angle of about 30 degrees to the side drain (Figure 18). But where a watershed crosses a dip (called a saddle) between two hills water will collect in both side drains at this point. Therefore a 'T' lead-off drain is taken off from each side at right angles, as shown in Figure 19. These drains do not have to be exactly opposite each other. Water approaches a 'T' lead-off drain from both sides instead of from one side only, as in the case of a normal lead-off drain.

The beds of these 'T' lead-offs drains are given a gradient of 1 in 125, or steeper. When excavating the drain all soil is carried to the road, and spread so as to raise the road along the lowest section,

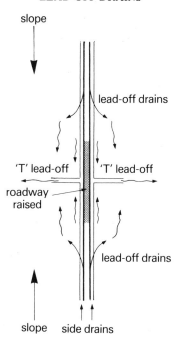

Figure 19. 'T' lead-off drains on saddle.

keeping it level. This means the 'T' lead-off drain need not be so deep and long.

4. Road Crossing A Gentle Saddle in Nearly Flat Country

Detailed survey (with a surveyor's level) on such a road may show that a long lead-off drain could remove standing water from the side drain. A better solution to the problem might, however, be to raise the whole length of road across the saddle, in the form of a low embankment, with no lead-off drain at all if the country is very flat. The road line must follow the exact watershed. This is a safer method than relying on one long lead-off drain, at a very slight gradient, to remove the water, especially if the area is likely to be cultivated. Such a drain might easily get blocked at one point.

5. Correct Spacing of Lead-Off Drains

It is not possible to state the correct spacing, nor can it be determined by a formula, if run-off from the bush is liable to reach the road at several places. Depending on this run-off the required spacing might vary from 20m to 200m or more. The overseer should decide by experience, noting carefully any evidence of the amount of storm run-off water reaching the road.

What really matters is the *volume* of water flowing in the drain: the distance between lead-offs is incidental.

CHAPTER 4
Drifts, Splashes and Culverts

1. Drifts and Splashes

A drift is where a road crosses a stream or river bed with the water flowing over the road. Splashes are very similar but on a much smaller scale, applying only to local run-off water which has to cross the road. Normally, they will be sited in slight natural depressions (watercourses) but if there are none of these and the ground is flat then they will have to be made artificially, for example, by making a dip in the high-level road.

The basic requirements for both drifts and splashes are very similar. In order not to inconvenience traffic the water must not flow deeply over the crossing. Furthermore, the crossing must be negotiable at reasonable speed by traffic when there is little or no water flowing across it.

A wide crossing with gentle slopes is therefore essential from both these points of view. A steep-sided narrow watercourse would make a very dangerous crossing for vehicles travelling at speed in the dry season. Moreover storm water in the rainy season would flow deep and fast, and this would inconvenience traffic and might prevent a drift being crossed.

In the interests of economy, gravel and stones must be depended on, in nearly all cases, for surfacing the crossing, concrete being too expensive. If there is a fast flow of storm water it will not affect concrete but it will soon scour out and wash away a gravel or stone surface. The speed of the water must therefore be reduced so that this does not happen. Grass often helps to bind the surface but it, too, will suffer if the rate of flow of the flood water is excessive.

In some streams which flood deeply the water will move only slowly; this is because the gradient on the stream bed below the crossing is slight. These deep, slowly moving floods do no damage at all to earthworks but the depth of the water will close the road to traffic (Figure 20(a)); this must be avoided if possible.

2. A Free Fall Reduces Depth of Flooding

In any watercourse, big or small, with only a slight gradient, a relatively large flow of water tends to bank up (i.e. flood deeply) because it cannot get away quickly (Figure 20 (a)). If, however, there is a raised roadway with a clear fall along its lower edge (Figure 20(b)), the water crosses freely over the fall and does not bank up; it remains shallow and vehicles are able to pass.

A quick get-away, i.e. rapid water flow, just below the crossing has much the same effect as raising the roadway; water will not tend to bank back deeply on the crossing. Whenever feasible, therefore, crossings should be sited at such spots in order to reduce the amount of embanking required. Rapid water results, of course, from the bed of the stream being on a steep gradient.

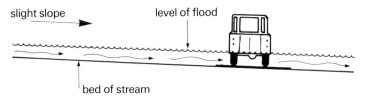

Figure 20(a). Slight gradient, deep flood.

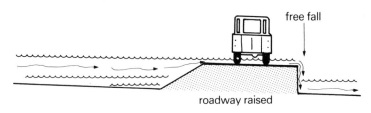

Figure 20(b). Free fall, shallow flood.

3. Widening the Crossing Reduces Depth of Flooding

If there is a free fall in both cases, the depth of flood in a wider crossing (Figure 21(b)) is much less than that in a narrow one (Figure 21(a)). The narrow crossing is more liable to hold up traffic and is also more likely to erode, owing to the greater speed of flow.

The two principles just discussed apply equally to both splashes and drifts. By applying them intelligently many difficulties, e.g. deep flooding in narrow streams, can often be readily overcome.

Figure 21(a). Narrow crossing, deep flood.

Figure 21(b). Wide crossing, shallow flood.

4. Stone-Filled Wire Gabions

A gabion consists of a heap of stones wrapped up and held in place by wire netting. It is often placed along the lower side of a drift or splash to support the gravel and stone filling and prevent it being washed away by flood water. This type of gabion is so heavy that only in exceptional circumstances would it be moved by a flood. It is cheap and easy to construct. One of its chief merits is that, if for some reason subsidence does occur underneath it, it will settle and block the cavity and no damage will be done. A concrete or masonry wall, on the other hand, would crack and perhaps collapse under similar circumstances.

As gabions are so inexpensive, drifts and splashes can be made as wide as practicable, in order to spread the flood. A flat stone apron may be necessary in order to prevent undercutting on the downstream side (Figure 22).

5. Culverts

Culverts are pipes that pass under a road to take storm water flow, rather than allowing it to flow over the road. They are normally situated where natural watercourses cross the road. However, culverts are sometimes placed at intervals along a road that runs slightly downhill across a long even slope to transfer storm water to the lower side of the road. Culverts are very expensive and are not

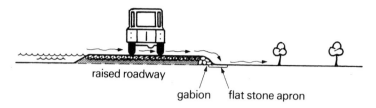

raised roadway

gabion   flat stone apron

Figure 22. Use of gabion.

warranted on village roads, only on market roads. The diversion bank alone is therefore depended upon to divert the storm water flow on a village road.

6. Types of Culvert
There are three main types of culvert that may be used:

1) Pre-cast concrete pipes.
2) Masonry construction.
3) Reinforced concrete construction.

The emphasis in this chapter is on concrete pipe culverts. However, if the necessary construction skills are available, and the costs are attractive, the other types may be used. There is, in fact, a fourth method of constructing culverts using wooden logs – these are cheap but do not have a very long life.

7. Flooding of Culverts
When any culvert is installed it must always be assumed that, sooner or later, it will overflow. It is often far too expensive to build it big enough to cope with the worst possible storm, and a culvert is also liable to become blocked with debris. Provision should therefore be made for emergency spilling of excess storm water over the road.

Blocked Culvert Pipes
Some culverts are at the bottom of a slope, where the road crosses a natural watercourse. There may be other culverts higher up the slope, where there is a long, gently sloping stretch of road with a crossfall but with no natural watercourse (Figure 23(a)). If the former type (culvert C in the Figure) becomes blocked the water will spill straight across the road to the lower side because the water

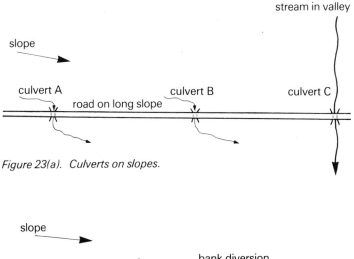

Figure 23(a). Culverts on slopes.

Figure 23(b). Use of bank diversion.

is confined to its natural valley and cannot go elsewhere. This type of blockage may cause a washout across the road, which is inconvenient but does no further damage and is easily mended.

On the other hand a blocked culvert further up the slope may result in very extensive damage. If culvert B blocks up, water will flow down the stretch of road from B to C which may become completely eroded. If culvert A blocks up, the road from A to B is likely to erode, and this in turn is likely to block up culvert B, so that BC also gets washed out. The damage done is far greater than that caused by any blockage at C. Except, perhaps, where there is a strong crossfall, hundreds of tonnes of soil may be lost on these long slopes and this will all have to be replaced.

This damage is easily avoided if a bank diversion, as in Figure 23(b), is constructed just downstream of the culvert pipe. Make use of any natural rise, so as to reduce the amount of fill required, by siting the culvert just on the upstream side of the bump.

Example of Safe Road Drift With Culvert
Figure 24 shows a stream crossing (similar to culvert C in Figure 23(a)) which is a combination of three rows of culvert pipes and a road drift held by a stone gabion, with emergency spillways. The hump of soil above the pipes in Figure 24 is necessary in order to protect the pipes from heavy traffic.

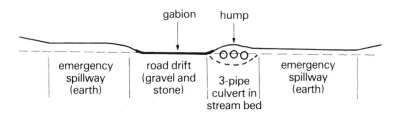

Figure 24. Side view of safe road drift with culvert.

The three rows of pipes are laid in the stream bed; this avoids having to excavate a run-out drain. They are 30cm, or more, below the level of the drift (i.e. the top of the gabion). If, during a sharp storm, the stream flow exceeds the combined capacity of these culverts and of the drift, the surplus flood can spill out over the grassed earth road on either side, as indicated.

The culvert pipes must not be too much below the level of the drift. One emergency spillway might be about 15cm higher than the drift and the other perhaps 15cm higher still. Often the two spillways can be on the same side making one long spillway sloping slightly, perhaps, from one end to the other. The lowest section could be made into the drift. It all depends on the convenience of the site. The longer the spillway can be made, the better.

The two ends of the gabion should rise slightly, say 15cm in 3m, in order to preserve the slight slope up required at either end of the drift (Figure 24). The length of the gabion for the drift will depend on the site and on the size of the stream when in flood. It is not unusual for the gabion to be 20-30m or more in length, with emergency spillways in addition, as an insurance.

High Flooding

If the behaviour of the stream when in full flood is not well known, consult local villagers. Ask them how high the flood has been known to rise, then imagine this flood (maybe 100m wide) flowing over the proposed road crossing. A flood covering the whole valley should do no damage to the earthworks, once they have grassed over, if the design is sound as in Figure 24.

There may, however, be a gully in the stream bed just downstream of the crossing and this could prove dangerous because flood water will drop down into it, which will tend to erode the side of the gully back towards the road.

The remedy for this is shown in Figure 25. Direction banks are made to prevent the flood flow from falling into the gully just below the crossing. For the same reason it is advisable to make these banks at every stream crossing where there is a culvert with a deep run-out drain. Gabions, anchored into the sides as shown, may be necessary in order to mend the gully if it is eroding due to heavy flooding.

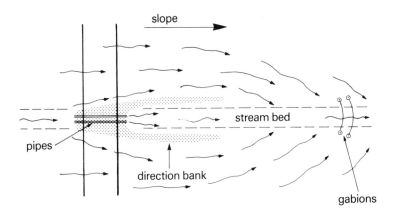

Figure 25. Use of direction banks.

Crossing a Stream Bed Subject to Severe Flooding

If the site is selected with care the flood may cause no inconvenience at all. The first essential is to be able to spread the flood over a sufficiently wide area of spillway, which will not erode or which can easily be protected from erosion. If the flood is not spread out, and the traffic is not to be held up, an expensive bridge must be built.

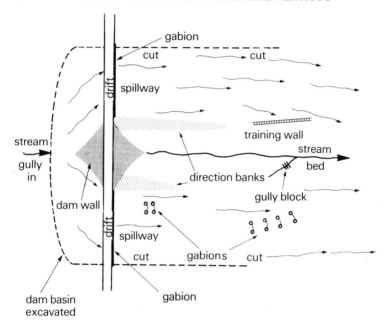

Figure 26(a). Complex crossing for severe flooding.

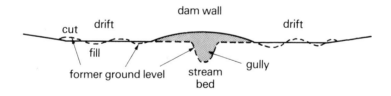

Figure 26(b). Side view of crossing along road.

The flood can be spread by dividing it in half as shown in Figure 26(a), (b). First the whole stream bed is searched until the widest possible crossing point is found. The stream bed is dammed, leaving maximum space for a spillway either side. A drift is constructed where the road crosses each of the spillways. Between them it runs up and over the dam wall. Direction banks (Figure 26(a)) prevent the flood returning directly into the stream bed.

The spillways will need some cutting and filling in order to give a wide, horizontal cross-section for some distance (Figure 26(b)). Gullies, etc, in the spillway could be protected with gabions, or blocked, as shown (Figure 26(a)). Training walls of heavy, loose rocks may be useful in order to encourage flood water to flow in the direction required.

The road runs over the top of the dam wall; if the spillways are adequate the wall need only be about 1m high.

Obviously this layout is only feasible if the valley is a suitable shape. The spillways should not need much cutting, and only a very little filling, to make them horizontal (i.e. horizontal at right angles to the line of flow). Any filled-in places should be consolidated.

The danger point, regarding possible erosion, is most likely to be where the flood drops down to the stream again; gully erosion is liable to eat back from this point to the spillway crest (in this case, the road). Prevent this, where necessary, with gabions (Figure 26(a)). It pays to discharge the water back into the stream at two or three points, instead of at just one point, in order to reduce the erosion liability.

From the foregoing observations it can be said that big floods in streams, and even in some rivers, can be negotiated satisfactorily (using only gabions and grass protection, without concrete work) if the floor of the valley is wide and flat enough to allow the flood to spread sufficiently. In narrow valleys the water cannot spread out. The flood will then run deep and fast, and, in consequence, any road crossing will have to be constructed in concrete which is very expensive; it is an engineer's job and is not considered in this book.

8. Run-Out Drains from Large Pipes

A 60cm culvert pipe needs 60cm of road soil on top of it to prevent it breaking. The bed of its run-out drain must therefore be 1.2m below the level of the road.

Where there is only a slight crossfall, if the road is not well embanked, a deep long run-out drain will be required (Figure 27(a)). These deep drains are expensive to dig and to maintain and they will give continual trouble in future years. Discharge from a similar pipe at a higher level on a well embanked road (Figure 27(b)) is much more satisfactory, and much cheaper, because the pipe is nearly resting on the surface of the ground.

The depth at which the culvert discharges can be reduced in two

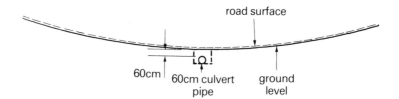

(a). Pipe below ground level, deep drain.

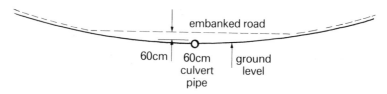

(b). Pipe at ground level, shallow drain.

Figure 27. Run-out drains from large pipes.

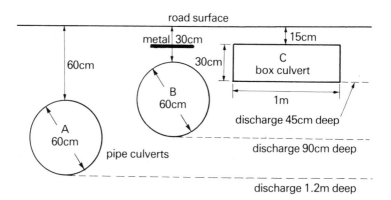

Figure 28. Methods of reducing depth of discharge.

ways. One way is to place a length of stiff metal, e.g. the tailboard of an old lorry, above the pipe as in Figure 28 type B. This protects the pipe from heavy traffic so that the soil cover can be safely reduced. The other method is to make a flat, reinforced concrete box culvert, type C in Figure 28, which only needs a thin covering of soil above it. Construction is, however, an expert's job.

CHAPTER 5

Precautions Against Silting

While it is easy to control erosion on earth roads by inexpensive conservation practices, control of silting is sometimes extremely difficult.

1. Types of Silting

Silt Deposited in Still Water

Silt-laden water flowing into a dam will, in time, fill it with silt up to the level of the spillway. In the same way a side drain will silt up to the level of the bed of its lead-off drain (Figure 29).

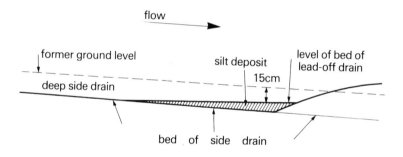

Figure 29. Cross-section through a silted side drain.

Silt Deposited by Running Water

If silt-laden water flows slowly through thick grass some of the silt will be deposited, even on a slope. The grass will grow up through the deposit and more silt will be accumulated. This can happen as a gradual process in a grassed side drain far above the level of its lead-off drain.

Sand Deposited by Uncontrolled Floods of Local Run-Off Water
When flood water gets completely out of hand and a series of
lead-off drain bolsters are washed away during a storm, the upper
reaches of the road will erode badly. At the bottom of the slope, if it
is fairly flat, long sheets of sand will be deposited in the side drains
and perhaps over the whole road too, obscuring it entirely. Most of
the coarser particles (sand and gravel) carried down by the flood are
deposited and the finer particles (silt and clay) are removed in
suspension in the water.

2. Remedies

Reduction of Silt Load in Run-Off Water Reaching the Road
Improved conservation agriculture and forestry above the road
does a lot to reduce the amount of run-off water, and the amount of
silt, reaching the road in small channels, etc. Often an easy way to
reduce the amount of silt, and the amount of run-off water, reaching
the road is to make diversion banks on all village roads, paths, cattle
tracks, etc. throughout the entire catchment in question. A very big
improvement is thus obtained at little cost.

Silting Due to Surface Wash Off the Road
If the surface of the road and side drain, etc., is washing badly it will
cause silting in the drains further down. Surface wash can be prevented almost entirely by allowing an earth surface to grass over.
This is why, in the high-level method, grass growth is encouraged
everywhere except on the carriagway itself, if it is to be graded
mechanically. On village roads the carriageway too is allowed to
grass over, since maintenance is normally by hand.

Catchwater Drains
When a gully, or small watercourse, meets the road, no damage is
caused if the flow of water is taken straight over, or under, the road,
as in Figure 10(a). Even if the water carries a heavy load of silt, it is
all washed straight across the road and away. No silting is caused in
the side drains. The damage occurs when the water is allowed to
flow along the road, as in Figure 10(b). The road erodes, or silts up,
or both.
    The principle should therefore be to prevent numerous small
gullies, etc. from discharging silt-laden water into the side drain

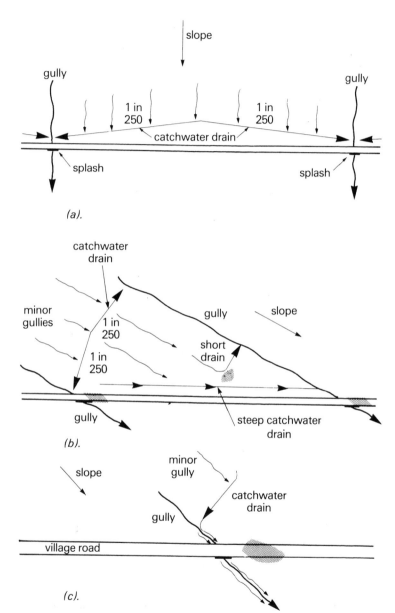

Figure 30. Catchwater drains.

(where the silt would be deposited) and, instead, to collect this water before it reaches the side drain and then to discharge it across the road at given points. It is collected by means of catchwater drains (Figures 30(a) and (b)). Figure 30(c) shows a similar catchwater drain protecting a 'flat' village road. As they are completely separate from the road, any erosion along the bed of the catchwater drains will not endanger the road itself.

A large flow of storm water requires a large catchwater drain to take it away but the gradient must not be too steep. A gradient of 1 in 250 should be all right but a steeper gradient may be allowed in gravels, etc. If only small flows are being considered, the drain can be constructed with a slope of 1 in 125. The steep drain in Figure 30(b) would probably be much steeper than 1 in 125 but it might be satisfactory in erosion resistant soils. If it carries a large flow of storm water, it will need one or more lead-off drains to divert water into the gully.

Lead-Off Drains

If much silt is carried in suspension in the water which flows in the lead-off drains, it will tend to deposit along the flatter stretches of these drains. Grass will grow through this deposit and more silt will then be held up. Soon the lead-off will cease to flow; the storm water will by-pass the intake bolster and will flow on down the road. Frequent maintenance is necessary to remove the successive deposits of silt if the lead-off is to be kept working. It is generally much cheaper to divert the silt, by means of catchwater drains, etc. before it reaches the side drain.

PART 2

Locating the Road

CHAPTER 6
Surveying

1. Selecting the Road Line

First make sure that all interested parties agree on the places to be linked by the road, and the standard required, i.e. market or village road.

Gradients

In the case of village roads it is as well to assume that they may be converted to market roads as the country develops. Steep gradients must therefore be avoided. In later years loaded lorries will be likely to use the road during the rainy season, and while they will not have difficulty ascending gradients of 1 in 18, a hill of 1 in 12 might cause wheel spin in the wet. On most soils an earth slope of 1 in 8 would prove impossible for a loaded lorry to climb in wet weather unless the surface was gravelled; but that is expensive. It is much better, therefore, to increase the length of the road somewhat if, by so doing, steep gradients can be avoided.

To upgrade a good village road to a market road is not an expensive operation (except on steep crossfalls) but to reduce a long gradient from, say, 1 in 7 to 1 in 10 means making a completely new road over that stretch; this is obviously very expensive. Always plan road lines, therefore, so that they will not have to be shifted in future years.

Watershed Road Lines

Cross drainage on a market road is either under the road (bridge or culvert pipes) or over the road (splash or drift); both are expensive. If a true watershed road line can be followed none of this cross drainage will be necessary; lead-off drains on both sides will conduct water away into the bush and this is cheaper than conducting it across the road.

Consider Figure 31. A road is required to run from point X to cross the stream. The best place for a drift is found at Y but the

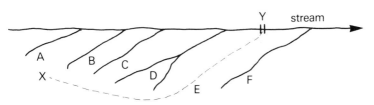

Figure 31. Watershed road line.

country between X and Y is unknown. To find the watershed route
between these two points start from the stream at Y and work
uphill; this will be route E. If a start is made, instead, from X the
watershed shoulders A, B, C, D and F might all be explored in error
before the correct route E is found.

Roads cannot always follow watershed lines. Consider Figure
32(a): this watershed consists of a rock ridge, impossible for any
road. A road from C to D will therefore have to pass below the
watershed, with a crossfall all the way. In Figure 32(b) the true
watershed route is undesirably long so a shorter line is chosen; this
route involves a stream crossing and stretches with cross drainage.

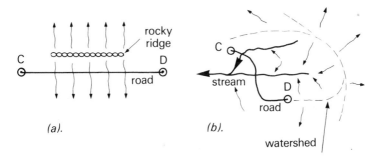

Figure 32. Roads not on watershed.

The cost per kilometre of these roads will inevitably be greater
than that for similar roads along watershed routes.

Straight Roads Desirable
Roads which twist and turn without good reason are not only a
nuisance, they are more expensive to maintain and may even be
dangerous. On sharp corners, high grass and tree growth on the

inside of a curve has to be cut down in order to reduce the risk of accidents due to poor visibility. Long gentle curves should therefore replace sharp corners wherever feasible.

Figure 33(a) shows another typical problem. To avoid the two streams the road must pass throught points A and B; this is a watershed line. The two points are reasonably near, but not too near, to the sources of the two streams, 1 and 2. Point C is the nearest point to the hill where the road can pass. Point D is the best site on the big stream for a drift where the road can cross. The road line ABCD is therefore satisfactory. The curves are gentle and the road cannot be shortened at all. Before deciding finally on point C, the possibility of a better road line round the north side of the hill (opposite to C) should be fully investigated. Another possible improvement might be to bend one of the straight lines AB, BC or CD slightly, if required, to keep exactly on the watershed; the merits of doing this would have to be considered.

In open country it is easy to peg a straight line by eye between two points A and B, etc. but in thick bush country an overseer is needed who can use a compass and plot a traverse, as described in the following section.

2. Traversing the Road Line

The overseer will need an oil-swung prismatic compass, a 50m tape or a cyclometer wheel[1], ruled or squared paper, a board to write on, a protractor, rules, pencil and flags.

The following example is given to illustrate the method. The overseer starts off his survey from point A in Figure 33(a) to cross the big stream D to the east some 9km away through unknown country. He is told of the hill near C so he begins his traverse by taking a reading of, say, 93 degrees on his compass (Figure 33(b)), hoping to pass just to the south of the hill. He walks on this bearing for 3.15km, at which point he finds he is approaching stream No. 2, so he stops. He decides to change direction and walk round the top of the stream (the source) so that he can get a watershed road line. He therefore sets off again, this time on a bearing of 11 degrees, walking upstream. The overseer stops at 0.7km and changes direction again to keep near the stream (No. 2); he then walks at 24 degrees on the new line and stops after 0.45km on this bearing. He

[1]A cyclometer is a standard bicycle wheel fitted with a simple device for measuring distances.

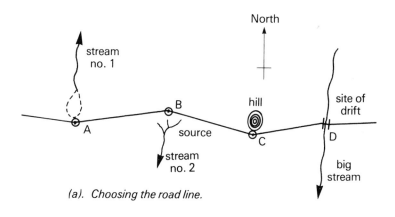

(a). Choosing the road line.

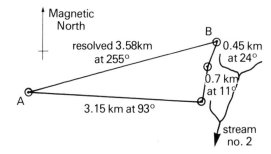

(b). Plotting the traverse.

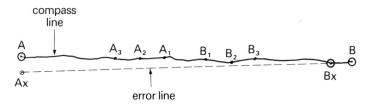

(c). Pegging the line straight.

Figure 33. Surveying the road line.

considers he has reached point B in Figure 33(a) which is where the final road must make a slight change in direction round the top of stream No. 2. This is point B in Figure 33(b). The correct road line should then be a straight line between B and A.

Plotting the Traverse and Resolving It

The overseer plots his traverse carefully on paper – from A, 3.15km at 93 degrees; 0.7km at 11 degrees; 0.45km at 24 degrees = B (Figure 33(b)). He then resolves the line BA which gives a bearing of 255 degrees (from B) and distance 3.58km. He then sets off from B on a bearing reading 255 degrees. He marks the line as he goes with flags and stops at 3.58km; this should be the point A. No doubt there will be some error, in which case he measures the distance and the bearing of this error line to reach A. If the error is big he may have to plot his traverse again, this time from B to A, then resolve AB, measure the bearing and walk the new line AB on the new bearing.

In the above example it is assumed that the final line AB is free of obstructions and is suitable for a road. If it is not, the best route must be found by repeating the procedures outlined.

Completing the Traverse

If the traverse ended at B then the line BA would be resolved immediately. However, if in the present traverse (Figure 33(a)) there is still some distance to go beyond B, the line AB is left till later. The overseer carries on from B traversing to C and on to D. Here he plots all his traverses resolving the lines AB, CB, DC.

He must make quite sure that the most suitable spot has been chosen for the drift over the stream at D. This might mean searching upstream and downstream for perhaps a kilometre or more. If a bad site is selected there may be major problems in future years. Some hours, or even days, spent investigating the relative merits of the different possible sites is time well spent.

The overseer walks back along the resolved bearing DC, one labourer marking the line behind him as he goes. If the whole line is suitable for a road and if it passes through, or near, point C he approves it and continues on from C to B on the new resolved bearing. If this too is suitable and passes near B he continues to A (his starting point) from B, again on the new resolved bearing which in this case is 255 degrees (Figure 33(b)).

Marking the Compass Line

This is the line trodden by the overseer reading the compass. The labourer following him marks the exact line with periodic cuts with a hoe and he also slashes trees adjacent to the line so that it can be found again without difficulty.

Pegging the Line Straight

The compass line will not be perfectly straight but will wander slightly. The line can be made straight using tall pegs with flags as markers.

Consider the compass line BA in Figure 33(c) which is about 3.5km long. Do not start pegging the line from one end, as in the case of the error line in Figure 33(c). Here a point Bx, exactly on the compass line, has been selected and a line from B through Bx has been projected to Ax; very large errors are likely to result from doing this.

Instead, start nearly halfway between A and B, (Figure 33(c)). Put in a tall peg A_1, with a flag, exactly on the compass line, in one of the hoe marks showing where the overseer trod. Go a short distance towards B and put in a similar peg B_1 also with a flag. Cut just enough trees along this line A_1B_1 to enable one flag to be seen from the other one. Move both flags outwards, to A_2 and B_2 (which are also on the exact compass line) and go on cutting in between so that they can be seen the one from the other. Move them outwards again to A_3 and B_3 and continue cutting in between to clear just enough for the line of the two flags to be seen.

This method could be continued until the whole line AB, is completed; alternatively, if the complete line of sight is obstructed by undulations in the ground, the line A_3B_3 could be projected both ways to reach up to A and B. In this way a perfectly straight road line is obtained.

Recording Obstructions Near Compass Line

In cases where the line may have to be shifted slightly, it is helpful to take note, in passing, of all rocks, gullies, huts and other obstructions near the line on both sides. By inserting this information on a plan, an improved line avoiding all obstructions can often be selected without a further exploratory survey.

PART 3

Construction Methods

CHAPTER 7

Construction of Market Roads

1. Pegging

The road line is first surveyed and pegged. Tall straight pegs, about 1·8m high, are inserted along this line at about 15-20m intervals. This will form the centre line of the road.

Next cut a straight 2·1m stick. Lay it down at each peg, at right angles (90 degrees) to the line, and hammer in a side peg at the other end of the stick (Figure 34). Repeat on the opposite side of the centre line. To get the right angle, stand at the peg on the centre line, look at the stick then look at the line, both ways; repeat two or three times, moving the stick as required. Take a new right angle for the second peg and do not just project the two former pegs. The two outside lines of pegs now show the edges of the 4·2m road (Figure 35(a)). The side pegs should be strong and about 1m high. They should be hammered in hard because they may have to remain in place for many months.

2. Dimensions of Road

This 4·2m road (pegged with the 2·1m stick) is the minimum for market roads. If preferred, a 2·4m stick, giving a 4·8m road, may be used. If the ground is liable to be at all damp, the 2·4m stick *must* be used. Use a 2·7m stick if the ground is liable to be wet and a 3·0m stick where it gets very wet. Where the road has to go through

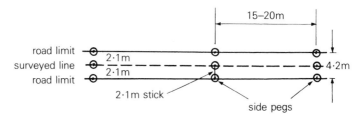

Figure 34. Inserting side pegs.

swampy ground with deep, soft mud and standing water, use a 3·3m stick (giving a 6·6m road, 13·2m overall including drains). For an important market road passing through wet swamp a 3·6m stick might be used.

The width of the road will therefore vary as the drainage problem varies. *The width of the carriageway, however, is the same for all earth roads,* namely 1·8m either side of the centre line, total 3·6m. This remains exactly the same whether the road is 4·2m or 6·6m wide. It is the width of the verge which varies, in this case from 30cm to 1·5m.

3. Stumping and Clearing

Every tree stump, big or small, alive or dead, must be dug out deeply by the roots. Encourage labourers to dig big holes so that the side roots can be cut further from the stump; they will then be less likely to shoot up again.

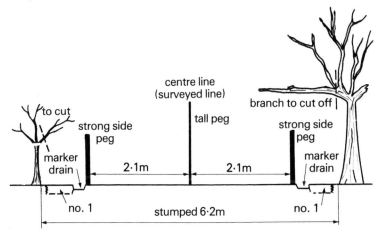

Figure 35(a). Clearing, stumping and marker drains.

On market roads stump to 1m outside the road limit on both sides (Figure 35(b)). The two lines of pegs will then be clearly seen. If there is one big tree just outside, or on, the line it might be allowed to remain, in order to keep down costs.

Some trees have stumps that can be burnt far down into the ground; this is the easiest way to get rid of them. If available, working cattle, or a tractor can be used to drag away the small

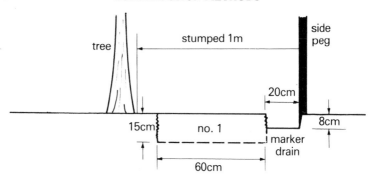

Figure 35(b). Extending marker drains.

stumped trees without further cutting up. Bigger trees will have to be cut so that the pieces can be pulled away one by one. Dump these in the bush well away from the road line. If branches of trees overhang the road at all they must be cut off (Figure 35(a)).

4. Rocks in Road
Dig out rocks and remove them, if feasible. If not, break them down to ground level, or lower, with a heavy sledge hammer. If necessary, make a hot fire on top of them for 2 or 3 hours, then remove the fire and ashes and immediately throw on plenty of cold water. The rock should crack and can then be broken easily with the heavy hammer.

Grass is probably going to grow on the verges of the road concealing any low obstruction, such as a rock, from drivers. This is potentially dangerous, and if it is not feasible to remove the rock or break it down to ground level, it should be permanently marked, e.g. by a white-painted iron stake, fixed so as to show above the grass.

After all trees, rocks, etc. have been removed, fill in all the holes, throwing off remaining sticks, and spreading all bumps. Hammer in all pegs again, keeping the centre line. A small 4-wheel drive vehicle should now be able to travel along either half of the road for inspection purposes.

5. Marker Drains
The two lines of side pegs, which show the road limits, must now be marked (Figures 34 and 35). One man can do this. He ties a string or rope between two of the side pegs and pulls it to lie straight. Standing on the string in order to hold it in place, he marks the line

of the string on the ground by scraping the line with a sharpened stick and having reached the peg he removes the string. Then, facing along the road, he takes a shallow cut (about 8cm deep) with his hoe, along the outside of the line made with the string, as shown in Figure 35(b). The marker drain is no wider than the width of his hoe, say 20cm. Swinging his hoe he throws the grass sods to the low spots in the road. He should move backwards, throwing the soil sideways. Trim the inside edge of the marker drain and leave it clean; this edge will be required in future. Leave the outside edge rough.

Both marker drains are dug, even on a steep crossfall. With the marker drains completed it is easy to see if any minor alterations in the road line are needed. Not much work is lost if, at this early stage, it is decided to shift the line a little; in this case new marker drains are dug.

6. Widening the Drains: No Crossfall

On hand-made roads the side drains, measured from the side pegs, should be as wide as, or wider than, the length of the stick used when pegging, e.g. a 4·2m road (pegged with a 2·1m stick) should have side drains 2·1m or wider. Figure 36(a) shows the final shape of the road.

The first main digging operation (No.1) consists of extending both marker drains outwards, digging 60cm wide and 15cm deep and throwing the soil to the road (Figures 35 and 36).

Use a stick 80cm long for checking the width measured from the peg line (20cm for marker drain plus 60cm for No.1 drain). The foreman must see that each labourer carries his own measuring stick 80cm long.

This No.1 operation should fill up all the places in the road, thus providing a reasonable running surface. Any high spots must be levelled without delay. Stumping was originally done to about 1m outside the road limit pegs so No.1 excavation is all within this stumped area (Figure 35).

The centre line of pegs should now be taken out so that traffic can pass over the whole road and compact it. More depressions will form, especially where the stumping holes were. No.2 operation is then done (Figure 36(b)). It is exactly the same as No.1 task, namely 60cm wide, 15cm deep, now measuring from the side peg line with a stick 1.4m long.

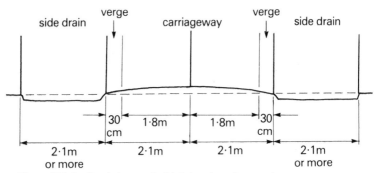

Figure 36(a). Final shape of a high-level market road.

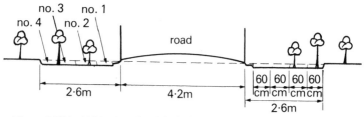

Figure 36(b). Widening the side drains.

Some trees may occur in this strip. All soil and grass is thrown to the road and levelled; small bushes, etc. are discarded, but bigger trees are left in place in the drain so long as they have not been loosened by the excavation. No.2 operation should provide a slight camber to the road.

No.3 operation (Figure 36(b)) should be done some months later when further inequalities in the road surface become visible. Dig as for No.1 and 2 but use a 2m stick, again measuring from the side peg line. As usual the labourer spreads the soil thrown to the road; at the same time any bumps must be cut down in order to get a good level running surface over the whole road. A lot of trees may be left standing in No.2 and 3 drains but they will not impede hoe and shovel work as it is easy to work between them.

No.4 operation could be done the following year (use a stick 2.6m long for measuring) by which time the road surface should be well compacted.

Each of the four operations is in the nature of a re-surfacing which fills in all the low spots. To put all this soil on in one operation is bound to leave a very uneven surface after traffic has consolidated it.

There is nothing to prevent an operation No.5, and even a No.6, being done if the road has to be enlarged at all.

7. Widening the Drains on Crossfalls

Normally the side drain will be about 15cm deep (Figure 35(b)). On steep crossfalls the side drain starts at this depth (upper side only) and increases across the width of the drain into the hill. Where there is a lower side drain (i.e. on slight crossfalls) the beds of the two drains should be level with each other, i.e. horizontal, as shown in Figure 37(a).

It requires skill to select this level correctly. Consider Figure 37(a). Excavation of the upper and lower side drains together provides enough soil to build the road up sufficiently, as shown. If one, or both, side drains are made a little shallower than in the Figure, then there will be little if any camber on the road (Figure 37(b)). If one or both side drains are made deeper than those in Figure 37(a) the road will be built up too much and labour will have been wasted. It will also be more difficult to remove water from this deep side drain.

Where the crossfall is a little steeper than it is in Figures 37(a) (b) and (c) no lower side drain will be required (Figure 37(d)), and only the marker drain is dug in the first instance. The level of the bed of the upper side drain is indicated in Figure 37(d). On steeper crossfalls the edge of the upper verge could be cut down (lowered) by about 8cm in order to reduce the amount of fill required for the road.

Another consideration is the height of the camber above the level of the beds of the side drains. It should be 30cm on flat and gentle slopes and a little more, say 30-40cm where the road has a steeper gradient.

The foreman must therefore be taught to select the correct level to which to dig the side drains. He must learn to be able to select the required height by eye; if he is supervising many labourers he will have no time to use his road tracer (see Appendix 1) on this work. After completion, check some levels by sighting with the road tracer from the bed of one drain across the road to the bed of the other drain. Check also the height of the crown of the road.

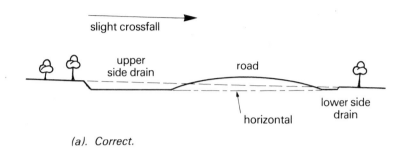

(a). Correct.

(b). Side drains too shallow.

(c). Side drain too deep.

(d). Steeper crossfall, lower drain not required.

Figure 37. Widening the drains on crossfalls.

8. Pegging of Lead-Off Drains

Refer to Figure 38. Method (a) is usually adopted, in order to save digging holes when pegging. For method (b) instructions are given to dig 15cm deep at the two marks, and in between as required, in order to give an even gradient (1 in 125). Boning rods (see Appendix 1) may be used to check the levels through uneven ground. Method (b) might be used to explain to new labourers the way to dig, and prevents errors due to undulations in the ground. The resulting drain is just the same as (a).

Method (c) shows how to find the run-out. The fall on the bed of the drains is still the same, i.e. 8cm in 10m or 1 in 125. Method (d), as in (a), saves the trouble of digging the hole (on the left) when pegging but it must be made quite clear to the labourer that he is to dig 15cm deep at one peg and nil at the other (at the run-out). These principles apply to the pegging of all drains.

9. General

Splashes and Culverts
These should be constructed where required as soon as the digging of the initial side drains (operation No.1) is finished. Occasionally a diversion bank may be required on a market road. This too should be built at an early date.

Regrowth
A lot of tree regrowth may occur during the first year or two after clearing; this should be dug out deeply and thrown away. Just to cut off the tops of the shoots will not stop regrowth.

Outward Slope of Side Drain
If water is allowed to stand in the side drain alongside the road, it may cause mud to form on the road. Side drains should therefore be dug so that they slope gently away from the road; water will then tend to stand far from the road and the carriageway will remain dry. This means that on a crossfall the upper side drain should slope slightly into the hill, i.e. away from the road. In the diagrams in this book the side drains are mostly drawn horizontal because the difference in slope is so slight.

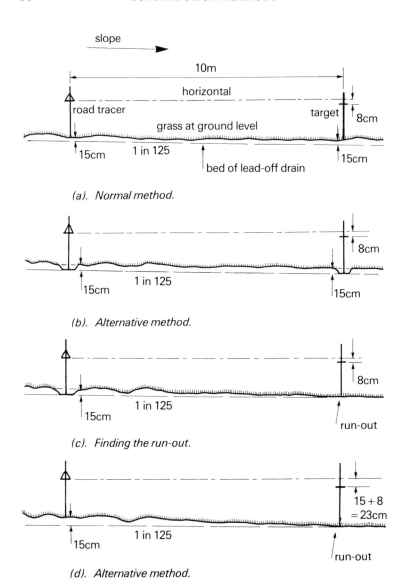

slope

10m

horizontal

road tracer

grass at ground level

target

8cm

15cm   1 in 125

bed of lead-off drain

15cm

(a). Normal method.

8cm

15cm   1 in 125   15cm

(b). Alternative method.

8cm

15cm   1 in 125

run-out

(c). Finding the run-out.

15 + 8 = 23cm

15cm   1 in 125

run-out

(d). Alternative method.

Figure 38. Pegging lead-off drains.

10. Construction of Embanked Roads in Wet Areas away from Stream Crossings

Normally the crest of the camber on a high-level road is 30cm above the level of any water that may be standing, or trickling, in the side drain. If water stands higher in the side drain, then the road must be raised (or the water level lowered) until there is the required 30cm of freeboard above the level at which the water is just flowing — called the full supply level (f.s.l.). These levels are obvious after rain. For this well-embanked road to be permanently stable, its sides must have gentle, as opposed to steep, slopes (Figure 39). The necessary 30cm of height could not be obtained with safety on a 4.2m road; a 6·6m road is the one required (refer to Section 2 above). (When an embankment higher than about 30cm is required, as at stream crossings in wet ground, steeper side slopes have to be adopted, in order to save expense.) Mark out in the normal manner, measuring 6m either side of the centre line.

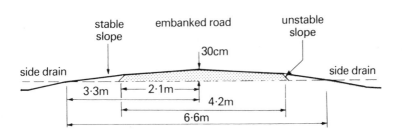

Figure 39. Embanked road in wet area.

Pilot Drains

If there is standing water on the site when work starts, dig a pilot drain, just like a marker drain (see Section 5 above): one hoe width and about 10cm deep, along this line of pegs on the outside (Figure 40(a)). Do not mark the line but dig the pilot drain straight by eye, watching the line of pegs. Throw the soil, including grass clods, etc. to the road. Each man works from the lower end of his task upwards, in order to avoid having to dig in standing water. This small drain will in time drain off the water and dry the ground.

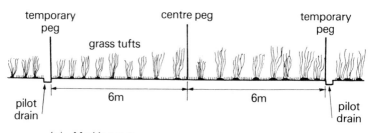

(a). Marking out.

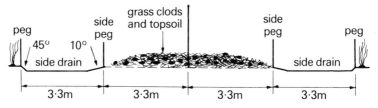

(b). Pegging and digging side drains.

(c). Compact surface.

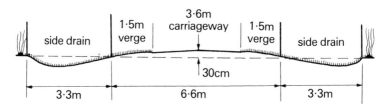

(d). Deepen side drains, increase camber.

Figure 40.   Construction of embanked road in wet area.

Pegging Road and Side Drains
Next peg the road limits exactly 3·3m either side of each centre peg (Figure 40(b)), using a 3·3m stick placed at right angles; put in strong pegs. Beyond each of these pegs put in another peg again 3·3m away, to mark the outer edge of the side drain. The pilot drain peg may now be removed. When fixing the 3·3m pegs at right angles in high grass, accurate measurement is easy if the line of the centre peg has been slashed and can be seen.

Digging Side Drains
Refer to Figure 40(b). Dig the side drains about 10cm deep and throw all the tufts of grass with the clods of roots and soil, etc. on to the road. Dig *under* the grass roots by working backwards from the clean area, especially if the grass is dense. The inner edge of the side drain is given a long gentle slope (about 10 degrees); the outer edge is steeper (about 45 degrees).

Lead-off drains must be inserted without delay, especially where long stretches of side drain are unprotected.

Surfacing the Road
Some levelling and compacting of the rough, uneven surface is essential at this stage if motor traffic is not to be seriously inconvenienced. The mass of grass clods, etc. on the road must now be consolidated as described in Section 12 below, and any high spots cut down as soon as they appear. An even, consolidated camber will soon form (Figure 40(c)). Clean soil is then dug from the side drains for surfacing the whole road and increasing the camber (Figure 40(d)). The drains are deepened more towards the outside, where the line of the pilot drain was originally.

Subsequent re-surfacing is done with more clean soil obtained by deepening the side drains. If much more soil is required the drains would have to be widened; in this case the grass roots etc. should be put on the verges and the clean soil on the carriageway. On crossfalls, widen the upper side drain and reduce the lower drain, as required.

11. Wet Ground at Stream Crossings
In section 10 above, the 3.3m stick gives an embankment about 30cm high in the centre (Figure 40(d)). At actual stream crossings, however, a higher embankment is often necessary. The gentle

outward slopes advocated throughout for market roads would be impracticable for these higher embankments so the following method is adopted instead. Keeping the same centre line throughout, the road is reduced from 6.6m (Figure 41, 'west side') to 3.6m, i.e. the width of the carriageway, in order to minimize the expense of the embankment. From both edges it slopes down at about 20 degrees (a gradient of about 1 in 3) to the bed of the drain. The carriageway is given a crossfall (downstream) of about 1 in 40, i.e. 9cm in the 3.6m, in case it is overtopped by the flood; water cannot then pond on the upper half of the road. (See also Figure 58.)

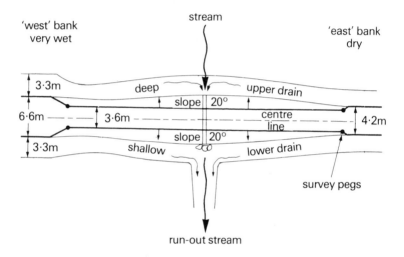

Figure 41. Plan of embanked road with culvert.

12. Consolidation

The main point of the high-level method is to raise the road by throwing on a lot of loose soil. This may inconvenience ordinary cars if it makes rough and heavy going. In these cases the initial consolidation should be done by tractor or jeep. A harrow or some sort of scraper will help to level the surface. Cattle pulling a loaded rubber-tyred cart do a good job, and often stone (for drifts and splashes) and gravel (for surfacing) can be carried, to advantage, at the same time.

Depressions should be filled in by scraping, etc. or by hand, throwing on more soil. A long rigid roller does not compact the small depressions at all whereas both wheeled traffic and cattle hoof action will do this well. Deep holes in the road are easy to deal with, even a well 3m deep full of water. Just fill it up with soil, etc. thrown in from outside, leaving a slight mound on top to begin with; keep on filling it in as it sinks. After a few months it will not be noticed at all.

Once the initial consolidation is completed the rest can be left for passing vehicles to do, by closing one side of the road to traffic. To employ special rollers, etc. to finish the job increases costs unduly. With mechanical construction the wheels of the tractor, etc. do most of the necessary compaction; it is only with hand-made roads that special means for consolidating the new construction may be called for.

13. Steep Slopes

Improving Gradients by Eye
Driving along a road one soon finds out which, if any, of the slopes are too steep. One can tell this without a road tracer, but this instrument is necessary if a new road line is being chosen in undulating country.

If a certain slope on an existing road is known to be too steep it is often possible to reduce its gradient at little cost, as shown in Figure 42(a). This can be sighted by eye, without any boning rods. All the low places are filled in and any excessively high places are cut off. In most cases the excavated soil can be used for filling. The amount of cut is decided by looking along the road with the eye in the correct position, as shown in Figure 42(b). More than one cut may be necessary. At the bottom of slopes it often helps if some filling in is done, as in Figure 42(c). In this case soil would be dug from the side drains, widening them. It is always a good principle to fill in the low places, where feasible, rather than to cut down the high places.

Removal of Water from Outer Side of Road on Steep Crossfall
Water may tend to flow along the road instead of being shed across the lower verge. This may be due to the presence of a small ridge in the carriageway or it may be due to eroded tracks. Where the accumulated water does escape to the lower side it will scour out a hole in the loose soil of the embankment.

In order to prevent this, the slope of the camber should be

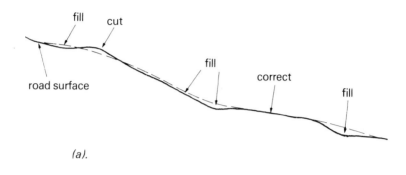

(a).

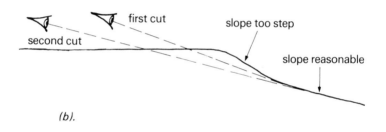

(b).

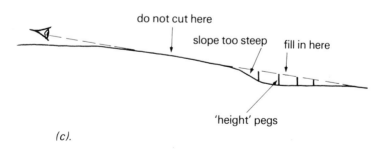

(c).

Figure 42. Improving gradients by eye.

maintained by filling in the tracks and grading (spreading the small ridge and any raised verge); alternatively, small inexpensive drains could be cut at close intervals to remove the water. No damage will be done if the water is run off before it is allowed to accumulate. The loose soil along the lower half of the road should be compacted by driving carefully near the outside edge, then resurfacing as necessary.

Upper Side Drains on Moderately Steep Crossfalls
When a market road crosses a steep slope it is generally impossible to make any lead-off drain at all along the upper side if the road is nearly on the contour. There is little advantage, therefore, in raising the level of such a road, so far as the lead-offs are concerned (the lower side lead-offs are easy, anyway). A *wide* upper side drain should be used. Widening the upper side drain is, however, not practicable on very steep crossfalls.

14. Gravelling
On the market roads considered here gravelling must be limited to drifts and splashes and to those stretches of road where the soil is particularly unsuitable, e.g. very light sand or heavy clay. For the most part they are ungravelled earth roads and hence cannot be expected to carry much traffic. Still less traffic is carried by village roads so, in the interests of economy, they have to depend on grass alone to stabilize their running surface; gravelling can only be afforded in exceptionally difficult places.

If it is necessary to gravel a stretch of road, do not bring in any gravel until the road had been raised to its full height by using the adjacent soil. If gravelling is done prematurely and the road has to be raised again later, this will mean covering up the expensive gravel.

Gravelling Embankments
If there is insufficient time, labour or money to raise the whole embankment and to gravel it all before vehicles must start using it a narrow embankment is first raised to the ultimate height required and then gravelled so that vehicles can just cross it at slow speeds, single file. Subsequently, when convenient, the drains are widened and the shoulders of the road filled in. This embankment then resembles that in Figure 41. No gravel is covered over.

Sand/Clay Mixtures

If gravel is expensive, because it has to be transported long distances, it may be cheaper to surface clay soils with sand and, conversely, very sandy soils with clay. The mixture can make a satisfactory running surface.

CHAPTER 8

Construction of Village Roads

Village roads are based on single lane traffic. The road is just wide enough for two cars to pass, but two lorries would have difficulty in passing where, for example trees are growing close to the road on either side.

1. Pegging and Stumping

Proceed in the same manner as for market roads (See Chapter 7, Sections 1 and 3) with the following exceptions.

(a) For pegging use a 1.8m stick instead of a 2.1m stick. This will give a 3.6m road. The width should be increased in wet places, and a small side drain dug.

(b) Stump to only 30cm beyond the side pegs.

2. Levelling the Road Surfaces

Since village roads are flat, with no camber or side drains, the road is simply levelled by cutting down all high spots (bumps) and filling in all low spots. High spots should be levelled as soon as they are observed, for if they are allowed to remain they may soon be compacted by traffic and become so hard that it will be very expensive to remove them. Any big grass tussocks in the road should be hoed up, as they can cause damage to vehicles. When soil is required for filling in low spots in the road, it should be dug from just outside the limit of the stumped area and thrown to the road. This digging can be regarded as the start of rough side drains.

The full stumped width (4·2m) should be levelled (Figure 43). When the side pegs have been removed traffic may utilize this full width of the road. Any mounds, etc. along the outside limit should therefore be spread on the road.

3. Diversion Banks

These should be started while the road is being constructed.

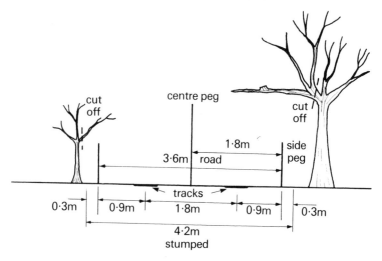

Figure 43. Dimensions of village road.

Pegging

The overseer selects the best site for each of the diversion banks and marks it out after first finding a suitable run-out (point B in Figure 44(a)). A road tracer (see Appendix 1) is essential for this work, except perhaps on steep crossfalls.

Refer to Figure 44(a). Stand with the road tracer in the middle of the road, at the point R where it is intended that the water will be diverted across the road. Make sure that the road tracer staff is held at the level ultimately required for point R when the work is finished. In some cases this will mean raising the present level of the road slightly at point R (e.g. if the road has been eroded much below average ground level and difficulty is experienced in finding a run-out) or it may mean making a small hole so as to lower the level of the point R. From R there must be a fall of about 8cm to average ground level at the run-out at B if the distance is less than 10m, or about 16cm if the distance is 20m, i.e. a fall of at least 1 in 125. If a steeper gradient can be found so much the better; the drain can then be shorter but B must always be a little lower than R so that water flows along the drain away from the road into the bush.

Strong pegs are used for marking out. One is fixed at B, then peg A is fixed near the road so as to give a good line for the drain. Peg C is fixed from the line AB on the opposite side of the road to give a

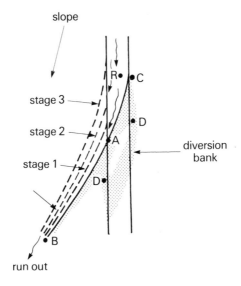

(a). Plan view.

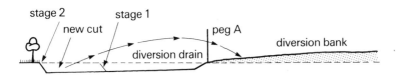

(b). Cross-section.

Figure 44. Pegging and digging diversion banks.

shallow curve. The line BAC will come a little below the point R. These three pegs A, B and C are hammered in hard and a mound dug round each to guard against the peg being removed by mistake. Mark the line AB then make a strong hoe cut at intervals along the line (standing facing the road) so that it can be easily seen. The position R is pegged only if the level is to be raised or lowered.

When pegging, the position of each bank must be clearly marked so that it can be seen from the position of the next bank along the road.

The overseer must be sure that the run-out water (from peg B) will not return to the road again. The path of the water can be quickly determined with a road tracer. The result of this check may well affect the choice of the site.

Digging

Dig a narrow, shallow channel along the upper side of the line AB (Figure 44(a)); throw all the grass soil etc. onto the road and spread it (Figure 44(b), stage 1). If B is far from the road, throw all the soil dug from near B as far as possible towards the road.

Widen this drain AB along the upper side, cutting the corner to reach the road (Figure 44(b), stage 2). Throw all this soil, etc. on to the bank in the road. Always move all soil towards the road in order to get enough to make a long, strong diversion bank. The cut line AB remains intact. All widening is done along the upperside of the drain; the lower side AB is not touched. Some filling is often required above the line AC, near C, in order to improve the shape (the curve) of the bank.

The bed of the drain must have a continous fall on it. In undulating ground therefore, it is no good digging it all the same depth throughout. Dig the drain deeper in the required places so that the water will flow. Towards the run-out end of the drain the depth gets less and less until ground level is reached at B. The bed of such a drain may be checked with boning rods (see Appendix 1); fix one at R (Figure 44(a)) and one at B and move the third in between.

Always start with a small shallow drain (stage 1) then increase it as required, widening and cutting the corner to give a satisfactory curve (stages 2 and 3). Water will tend to flow along the upper side of the drain so its bed should be sloped slightly into the bank. The crest (summit) of the diversion bank (DD) will have to rise nearly 30cm above the level of the road at point R if storm water is not to overtop it.

If more soil is required on the bank cut more off the corner and widen the drain; do not get it by digging holes in the bush. A wheelbarrow is sometimes required for finishing off long diversion drains so that the soil can be brought to the road.

Where there is little traffic it is worth running a motor vehicle repeatedly backwards and forwards all over the new bank to compact it and then surface it again where required. The overseer in charge should travel along the road by car or lorry to see how his banks 'feel' and perhaps, how he can improve them.

The levels of the completed work should be checked and this is simply done as follows. Stand the road tracer at R and see that there is a fall of 8cm or more, to the run-out at B; also that there is a rise of nearly 30cm from R to the top of the diversion bank DD.

4. Wet Areas

In well-drained upland country a flat village road is much cheaper than a high-level road. In wet areas, on the other hand, there is little difference between the two. Loaded lorries should be able to use any village road throughout the rainy season, including roads in the wet areas.

The high-level type of construction is therefore essential in wet areas for both market and village roads; no economy is possible in the case of the latter.

CHAPTER 9

Construction of Splashes, Drifts and Culverts

These are constructed, as required, on both village and market roads.

1. Splashes

Shape

The flat V-shape (Figure 45(a)) is dangerous if taken at speed and should not be used. All splashes should have a flat base 2-3m wide (Figure 45(b)), with gently sloping approaches. This splash is wider than (a) but not so deep; its flow capacity is about the same as (a). This is referred to as the standard type of splash. Figure 45(c) shows a splash which is the same depth as (b) but much wider; it therefore has a greater capacity and it can be taken much faster in comfort. This improved type (c) may be merited on the bigger splashes and drifts on the more important market roads. An overseer should be able to lay it out himself unaided, as described below.

It will be easy to lay out the standard splash with a road tracer if the layout of the improved splash is first understood.

Improved Splash

This is explained in Figure 46. Insert the sixteen marker pegs according to Figures 46(a) and (b). At the side of each marker peg, on the line, hammer in a height peg (see Appendix 1) as in Figure 46(c). Make them all, say, 15cm higher than the intended height of the ultimate road surface, so that they will show well above the road surface when the work is finished. The road surface should be given a slight downward slope in the direction of water flow.

When first pegged, the A pegs in the bed of the splash (Figure 46(c)) will in most cases be below the original ground level. Therefore dig a hole, as shown, so that the pegs can be easily seen. A lot of excavation will be required at these pegs during construction. Some excavation will probably be required at pegs B and some filling in at

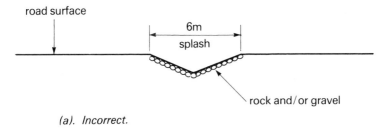

(a). Incorrect.

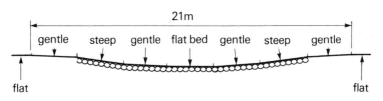

(b). Standard splash.

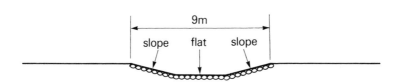

(c). Improved splash.

Figure 45. Cross-sections of splashes.

pegs C. A lot of filling in will be required at pegs D (Figure 46(b)).

The lower portion of the splash will be lined with rock and/or gravel (see Figure 45(a)). The layer will be about 15cm deep so the ground must be excavated to this depth to make room for it (Figure 46(d)). Refer again to Figure 46(b). Use of a 5cm vertical unit would give a shallow splash only 20cm deep (because there are 1+2+1=4 vertical units). In this case a small bank diversion is advisable in order to give the required 30cm freeboard on the

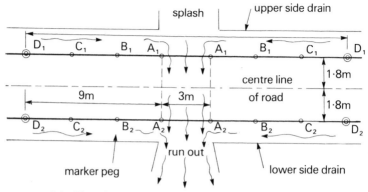

(a). Plan view.

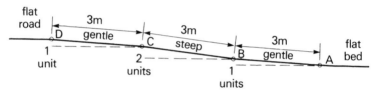

(b). Side view of final shape.

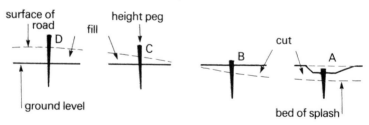

(c). Use of height pegs.

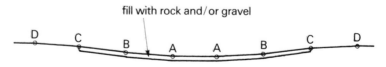

(d). Excavation for rock/gravel lining.

Figure 46. Construction of improved splash.

downstream side. An 8cm unit would make the splash 8×4=32cm deep and a 10cm vertical unit would make it 40cm deep. The deeper the splash, the greater its capacity. For higher speeds, especially on these deeper splashes, the 3m measure used in Figure 46(b) could be increased to a 4m or even a 5m measure.

Standard Splash
This type of splash (Figure 45(b)) has a flat bed 3m wide, with gently sloping approaches at a uniform gradient. It is easier to construct than the improved splash, but the general method is the same. The approaches may have to be steepened in hilly country.

Run-Outs From Splashes
In flat country splashes must be raised up (see Figure 20) so that there is a free fall, or nearly free fall of about 20cm, for the water passing across the splash and down over the gabion. This will reduce the liability to deep flooding on the splash itself. Even if the whole run-out area, and the apron, are just under water the splash should still discharge unimpeded. Water must only spill over the road at the splash so make sure that all the rest of the road nearby is high enough above the level of the splash.

Where there is a slight crossfall it is economical to excavate a little all along the lower side of the gabion, as shown in Figure 47, the soil going to raise the road. If, say, a 10cm depth is excavated, the road need only be raised 10cm above ground level to give the same 20cm fall as before. If the embankment is long this reduction in height will mean a big saving in labour.

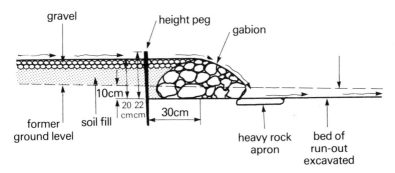

Figure 47. Construction of gabion.

If water will flow away naturally from the splash (i.e. there is a definite crossfall) without any risk either of gullying or of gravel being washed off the splash, then there is no necessity to build a gabion for protection. However, a cheap gabion might be laid to define and mark the shape of the splash.

Building a Gabion

The amount of fill required on the road will depend on the height at which the gabion is built (Figure 47). Be careful, therefore, to select the correct height for the gabion pegs so that the amount of fill required on the road will equal the amount of excavation necessary to complete the run-out, the lower side drain and the upper side drain (see Figure 46(a)). Soil excavated near the lowest point of the splash (A in Figure 46(a)) is, of course, moved uphill (towards D) where a lot of filling is required.

Figure 47 shows the construction of a gabion with a slight crossfall. A wide trench is first excavated along the required line for the gabion to a depth of about 10cm. Height pegs are then driven in about 30cm from the centre line of the proposed gabion, on the upstream side, until they are all 2cm above the level required for the splash. Holding a 22cm stick, measure down from the top of the peg, excavate as required and make a mark. Do this at one metre intervals using boning rods or sighting along the top of the pegs. Then complete the excavation of the trench.

The required length of 12-gauge diamond mesh wire netting (a strip 1.3m wide will make a gabion 20cm high) is laid along the prepared ground slightly off centre (Figure 48(a)). The stones are laid in a long heap along the netting, and the sides are folded over and tied together (Figure 48(b)). Thinner 16-gauge wire can be used for tying and it is fairly easily bent with the fingers, but thicker 14-gauge wire may need pliers to bend it. Cut the wire into short lengths and tie each knot separately. Then fill in with soil and finally gravel on top, as shown in Figure 47. The pegs will all show 2cm above the road surface. A rock apron should be laid on the downstream side of the gabion (Figure 47) to prevent the falling water from undercutting the gabion.

In some places box gabions may be purchased ready-made. A box gabion is a wire netting box which is laid in position and filled with stones. The top of the box is then tied to the sides with wire (Figure 48(c)). Various shapes and sizes of box gabion can be obtained. A

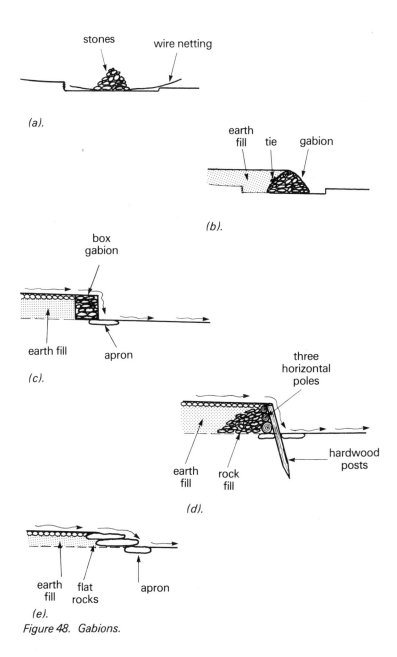

Figure 48. Gabions.

second or third layer may be added on top of the first, if required.

If gabions cannot be made, hardwood poles can be used (Figure 48(d)) but they will be liable to rot. They are held in place by posts driven in, at intervals, into the stream bed.

If big, flat, heavy rocks are available they can be laid as shown in Figure 48(e). They will act like a gabion if they are heavy enough for storm water not to move them.

Warning Marks

Drivers must not travel over the splash unduly fast, so warning signs should be erected. Tall poles painted white, at either end of the gabion and in line with it are suitable (Figure 49).

Farm implements and road grader blades, etc. must be kept clear of the wire netting. To ensure this a long stone should be fixed upright at each end of every gabion, in line with it, and sunk into the ground to make it firm (Figure 49). Choose a white stone or paint a stone white.

Splashes to be Sited on Straights

The surface of the road at a splash should normally slope down the hill, but a corner or bend in the road should slope inwards. In Figure 50(a) the slope on the splash is down the hill whereas the slope on the two corners is into the hill. In Figure 50(b) it is impossible to satsify both these requirements at the splash. If a culvert is installed in place of the splash then this complication does not arise.

Splashes Crossing Gullies, etc.

Where the road has to cross a gully or other depression, it may be necessary to raise the splash more than 20cm above the bed of the gully. This is easily done by laying two or more gabions as shown in Figures 51(a) and (b). This principle means that splashes can be laid, if necessary, at any desired level, irrespective of the existing ground levels.

Splashes Diagonally Across Road

A splash can be made at any angle across the road (Figure 52) instead of straight across it at right angles. This may be desirable where there is a gully, for example, so that the splash follows the line of the gully. The top of the bank diversion should be 30cm above the

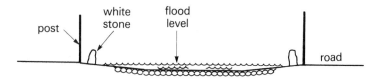

Figure 49. Warning marks at ends of splash.

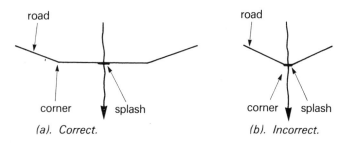

(a). Correct.   *(b). Incorrect.*

Figure 50. Splashes to be sited on straights.

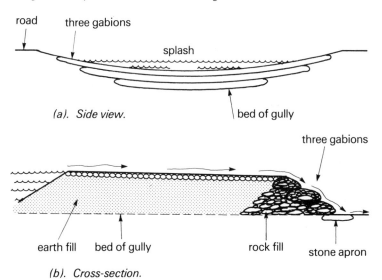

(a). Side view.

(b). Cross-section.

Figure 51. Splashes using more than one gabion.

bed of the splash so, if the gully is 30cm deep, the height of the bank need not be increased at all.

Splashes in Flat Country
These need careful surveying with a surveyor's level. The principle is exactly the same as for ordinary splashes; all the flow of water must be diverted, even in the worst storm, and it must not return again to the road below. This is achieved by constructing retaining banks.

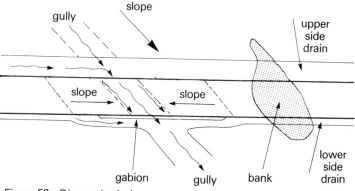

Figure 52. Diagonal splash.

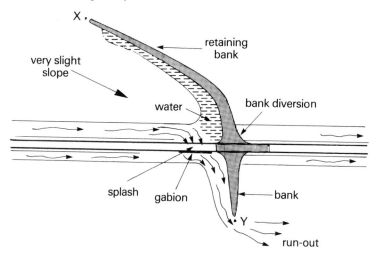

Figure 53. Splash in flat country.

Refer to Figure 53. If the water flows nearly 30cm deep on the splash (upper edge) during a bad storm then the point X (which is at ground level at the top end of the long retaining bank) must be 30cm or more higher than the splash. If it is less than 30cm above the splash some of the storm flow would probably pass round the top end of the long retaining bank and would reach the road again. To prevent this the retaining bank is continued up the hill until the point X, at its tip, is high enough.

The splash must, as usual, have a free, or nearly free, fall along its lower edge. From the apron there must be a slight gradient all the way to the run-out at Y (Figure 53), preferably not flatter than about 1 in 400. In flat land it is generally necessary to excavate the entire bank, from the apron to the run-out point Y. This bank must be lengthened if it is suspected that the flow may find its way back to the road further on. Make this bank at right angles to the road.

Decide the level of the splash with care. The higher it is, the longer the upper bank will have to be; the lower it is, the longer will the bank on the lower side have to be. These banks may be more than 50m long in flat country, so each splash is expensive. They should therefore be spaced wide apart, perhaps up to a kilometre and this means that very wide, shallow side drains will have to be made in order to accommodate the increased flow arising on these long, uninterrupted stretches of road.

A standard splash with the 3m flat bed (Figure 45(b)) would be too small to deal with large flows of storm water. The 3m level bed must be increased to 10-15m so that the splash can never flood more than 30cm deep. This splash will look like Figure 54 when viewed from the lower side drain. With a fall of about 20cm over the gabion a splash of this length, will dispose of a very large flow of water when it is running nearly 30cm deep.

The approaches to the splash in Figure 54 have gentle slopes of

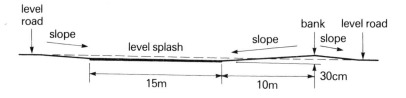

Figure 54. Standard splash in flat country.

about 1 in 30 (30cm in 9m) which means that it can be taken at speed in a car. This long, level splash must be levelled carefully. This is best done with boning rods.

2. Drifts

The construction principles for drifts (in rivers and streams) and for splashes (at minor flows) are basically the same, so they will not be repeated here.

More than one gabion may be laid, as in Figure 51, if a good drop is required. Alternatively a bigger gabion can be built using 2m or wider diamond mesh wire netting in place of the standard 1.3m width. If the drift has to cross a depression in a river bed it could be filled in as shown in Figure 51. Normally the top of the main gabion should be level throughout, except for the turn-up at either end where it is let into the bank.

Laying Rock Paving at Stream Crossings

At crossings where the water will never flow fast, a surfacing of gravel will provide sufficient protection, as described in the previous section.

Where fast-flowing storm water may be expected, rocks should be laid flat, or preferably on edge, as shown in Figure 55(a) and (b). To do this, first insert height pegs to show 2cm above the surface, spacing them 2-3m apart. Then use a straight edge plank or string along the tops of the pegs and lay the rocks 2cm below it. Pack the rocks together tightly in the soil then fill up the surface gaps with good soil and plant a short creeping grass.

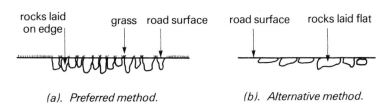

rocks laid on edge   grass   road surface   road surface   rocks laid flat

(a). Preferred method.   *(b). Alternative method.*

Figure 55. Rock paving.

Utilising A Rock Bar

If there happens to be a low, solid, rock ridge in a suitable position the spillway can sometimes be made to discharge over it; there will then be no erosion risk at all. This is shown in Figures 56(a) (b) and (c). Gaps in the rock can be filled in with concrete (ask advice) or gabions. Deep gullies may eat back up to the foot of the rock bar but they can go no further.

The road can be at the rock bar (Figure 56(a)), or it can be some way upstream of it (Figure 56(b)) with a retaining bank; many variations are possible.

When flood waters from dam spillways discharge over grass on a slope there is always a risk of the water concentrating and causing gullies. The drop should all occur at a waterfall, over immovable rock, and not over a grassed slope on erodable soil.

If the rock bar lies across the stream bed, as in Figure 56(c), instead of to one side, as in Figures 56(a) and (b), the gaps between the rocks are filled in and the road is taken straight across. This is the easiest and cheapest type of crossing but suitable sites for this method are not often found.

With a rock spillway there is no need to divide the flood but in the case of grass spillways every effort must be made to spread the flood and so to reduce the risk of damage at any one point.

Safeguarding Bridges

Occasionally, tree trunks, etc. float down the stream when it is in flood. These may be washed against a bridge, in which event more debris is likely to collect and this may cause a complete blockage. The full flood then has to go over the top and part, or all, of the bridge may be washed away. In many cases it is possible to guard against this. Consider the two sites in Figures 57(a) and (b).

In (a), flood water has to pass under, or over, the bridge. It cannot go anywhere else. If a blockage occurs, the flood will pour over the top of the bridge in a free fall, seriously damaging even a concrete structure. In (b), the main flood can by-pass the bridge if a serious blockage does occur. All the water can get away over the low level drift on the left without causing any damage to the bridge. If this drift should breach a few tonnes of soil will put matters right. Make sure that the spillway level is well below the underside of the bridge deck.

3. Construction of Culverts

There are numerous ways of designing stream crossings with culvert pipes. In fact, each crossing presents a different problem.

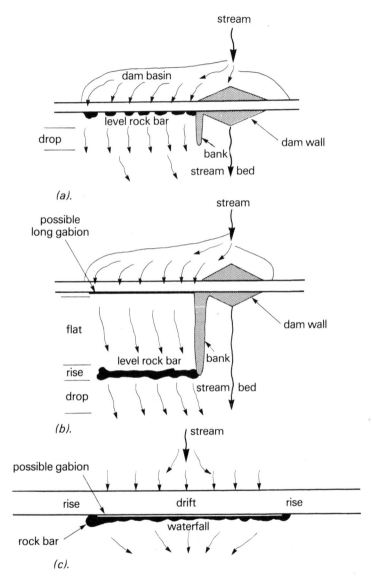

Figure 56. Utilising rock bars.

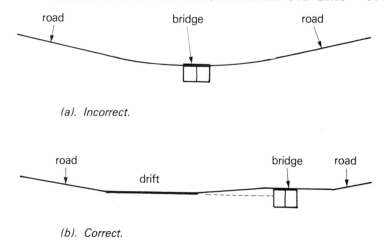

(a). Incorrect.

(b). Correct.

Figure 57. Safeguarding bridges.

Example

Figure 41 shows a plan view of a typical culvert arrangement, and Figure 58 is a cross section through it at the stream crossing.

In Figure 58, the ground has a crossfall of 1 in 20 from the left. A 30cm culvert pipe is shown; in this case it is 8m long. Its outlet is 16cm lower than the inlet, i.e. a slope of 1 in 50, in order to prevent silting inside the pipe. The carriageway is given a crossfall of 1 in 40, i.e. 9cm in 3·6m, in case of flood, and its centre is 50cm high (above former ground level) i.e. 20cm higher than the camber of the wide high-level road which approaches the crossing from the 'west' (see Figure 41). The soil cover above the culvert pipe is about 45cm. This is only just enough to prevent heavy lorries breaking the pipe if it is made of concrete; 60cm soil cover would be safer.

Another important point to watch is the amount of freeboard, that is, the vertical height of the road above the level of the water standing in the drain (the f.s.l.). In the above case (Figure 58) the freeboard is 75cm (measured from the bed level of the pipe intake to the level of the upper edge of the road). If the freeboard is less than 30cm the surface of the road may get damp and turn into mud.

When digging the upper drain the soil will have to be thrown about 7m on to the road. This is not at all difficult so the drain could be widened if necessary (or deepened as indicated in Figure 58).

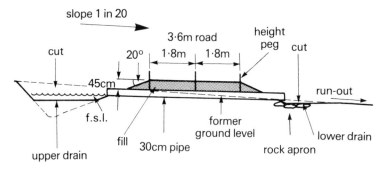

Figure 58. Cross-section through culvert.

Short crossings can be pegged with a road tracer but for longer crossings an accurate surveryor's level will be necessary.

Survey Pegs
Before deciding on the exact layout, survey pegs should be inserted to show the proposed dimensions of the work, e.g. the positions of the top and bottom of the culvert pipes at both ends (inlet and outlet), also the length of the run-out drain (if any) and the height of the embankment and its length, as shown by the point on each bank where the level road meets the rising ground (Figure 41).

To get an idea of the amount of work involved in digging the embankment, first fix two low survey pegs at both ends of the embankment, one for the upper and one for the lower edge of the road; the tops of these survey pegs indicate the designed levels. Fix three or four similar pairs of survey pegs at intervals along the embankment by sighting by eye along the tops of the pegs. Choose pegs of suitable length and hammer them in until their tops show level. Guess a 20 degree slope (outwards) from the tops of each of these survey pegs and put in a stick where this slope meets the ground (Figure 59); this will mark the edge of the upper drain which is also the toe of the embankment. Do the same along the lower side.

This rough survey will help the overseer to decide whether to start construction or to improve on the proposed layout before starting.

Height Pegs
When the embankment is completed the survey peg will be very

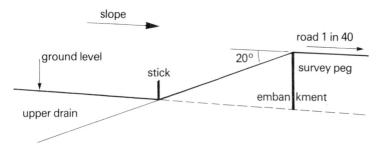

Figure 59. Use of survey peg.

nearly, if not quite, covered with soil and will be difficult to see. Height pegs will therefore be required.

It is impossible to decide on the exact height required for an embankment until the work on it is nearly finished. The completed bank may exceed the designed height or it may fall short of it. The height pegs should therefore be inserted so that they will still show slightly above soil level however high the bank is made. A margin of 25cm for the height pegs above the designed level is generally enough. The pegs will then all show exactly 25cm if the embankment is finished exactly as designed. If the embankment is finished 8cm short of the designed height then all the height pegs will show $25 + 8 = 33$cm above the soil at the finish; on the other hand, if the designed height is exceeded by, say, 15cm, all the height pegs will show $25 - 15 = 10$cm above the soil. All height pegs will still be readily seen and none will be covered over and lost.

Building the Embankment
It is important to raise the embankment equally throughout; do not complete one section, leaving the rest until later. When the whole embankment is about half built insert height pegs between the survey pegs at roughly 2m intervals, in the positions shown in Figures 60(a) and (b); by waiting until some soil has been built up, shorter height pegs can be used (Figure 60(b)). They must be firm and accurate.

One labourer is then detailed to make up the soil level around each height peg. To begin with, give him a measuring stick say about 40cm long, as in Figure 60(c). Measuring down from the top of the height peg he builds a firm mound at that level. He could do 50 pegs

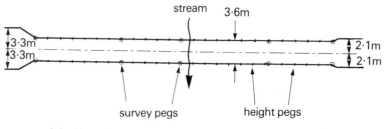

(a). Plan view.

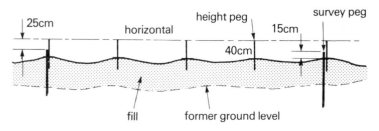

(b). Side view.

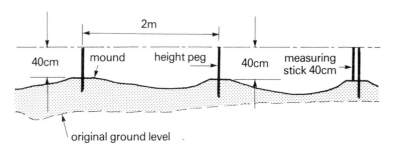

(c). Marking the level.

Figure 60. Use of height pegs.

like this in 2 or 3 hours. These initial mounds will be 15cm below the designed level of the embankment, which is shown by the level of the survey pegs (Figure 60(b)). As usual the height pegs stand 25cm above this level.

Filling in the embankment continues up to the level of the mounds. It may then be decided to raise the embankment a little more, say 10cm; this would make it only 5cm short of the designed level. The same labourer raises all the mounds again, this time using a 30cm stick. This height might prove adequate; on the other hand some further final cutting and filling might be necessary, in which case the whole embankment might be raised again by another 15cm, say. This would raise it 10cm above the designed level so that a 15cm stick would have to be used at the height pegs when making the mounds. This work is easy once the principle is understood. Fixing the height pegs 25cm above the designed level is alright for the larger embankments but for low embankments 15cm would do.

During the later stages of construction, traffic should run frequently all over the earthwork in order to compact it well. Top it up finally some months later.

Position of Culvert Pipes

The overseer must choose the most suitable layout after considering all possible alternatives.

Figure 61 shows a side view of a road embankment where it crosses a stream. The flow will pass under the road through a 60cm culvert pipe, four possible positions of which are illustrated and described in order of preference.

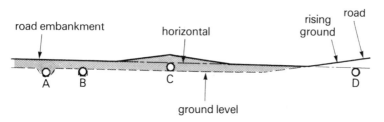

Figure 61. Position of culvert pipes.

	Freeboard on main embankment (cm)	Soil cover above pipe (cm)
(a) Pipe in gully	120	60
(b) Pipe in trench	120	60
(c) Pipe at ground level	60	60
(d) Pipe up hill	60	60

(a) The pipe is laid in a naturally gullied stream bed, if there is one. If it is deeper than 60cm so much the better but it must not be too deep. The run-out drain is ready-made and its cost is *nil*.

(b) A trench 60cm deep is dug to take the pipe. A run-out drain is also required. In flat country this drain may have to run for hundreds of metres and this may make the cost prohibitive; in this case adopt method C below.

(c) The pipe is laid on the ground and the embankment is raised 60cm above it. The water will discharge over the grass; cost of run-out *nil,* even in flat country. Either a bump is left in the road, just above the pipe, as shown, or the whole embankment is raised 60cm to make the road level. The latter is expensive, especially on long crossings. On the other hand a bump in a market road is a nuisance to traffic and, more important, if the 60cm of soil cover over the pipe is reduced unduly by repeated grading, the concrete pipe may break under heavy traffic.

(d) This method is rarely used. Pipe laid in rising ground beyond end of embankment, hence no bump in road. As in C, water will discharge at floor level. Only merited where the gradient of the valley is very flat and where the road at D follows down a sharp watershed (or between two gullies) so that cost of excavation up to the pipe (in both side drains) is not excessive.

Provision for Flood Water

As stated in Chapter 4, Section 7, culvert pipes can seldom cope with the full storm flow of a stream. Periodically the flood will reach the top of the embankment and so provision must be made for the water to spill safely over the road in an emergency.

Long, low embankments that are horizontal from one end to the other, with a well-grassed gentle slope on the lower side, should give no trouble when overtopped by a high flood. Higher embankments will be dangerous if the flood flow can concentrate at a weak spot. In such cases a definite portion of the embankment should be selected as a spillway where it can be seen that no damage will occur; this is shown in Figure 62(a). If the flood overtops the embankment directly above the deep stream bed the result would be serious but, thanks to the presence of the emergency spillway, the flood should do no damage at all (see also Figure 57(b)).

The spillway is made nearly 30cm lower than the main embankment and simple protective measures may be needed below it, e.g. levelling off and filling in, in order to spread the flood, together with, perhaps, a low earth direction bank and gully protection. All

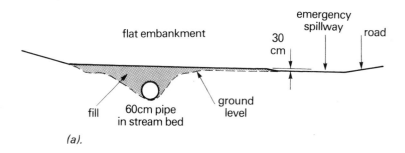

(a).

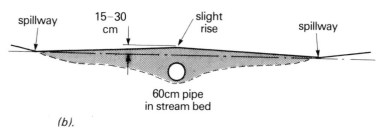

(b).

Figure 62. Use of spillway for flood protection.

these works would, together, represent only a fraction of the cost of installing further culvert pipes in an attempt to prevent the embankment being overtopped by storm water. The spillway can be constructed in the form of a drift or a long road splash; see Sections 1 and 2 above for details.

In Figure 62(a) the obvious place for the spillway is on the right-hand side, as shown; there will be little or no fall from the spillway down to ground level at that point.

In the case of Figure 62(b), however, there is no ready-made place for a spillway. In such cases the flood must be encouraged to spill where it is safest, i.e. at either bank, where there is no drop down to ground level, rather than in the centre above the stream bed where there is a high drop and soft soil. To do this, the road directly above the deep stream bed is raised an extra 15-30cm, as shown. Simply insert a peg 15-30cm up, sight to the horizontal pegs at either end of the embankment, adjust the pegs in between with boning rods (see Appendix 1, Figure A6) or by eye (see Figures 42(b) and (c)) and fill the embankment up to the new line.

Inadequate Soil Cover Above Pipe
It was explained earlier that the 45cm of soil cover above the pipe under the road could be increased to 60cm (or more) to advantage, in order to reduce the risk of breakage (see Figure 58). There are two ways of doing this. One is to raise the level of the embankment 15cm; the other way is to lower the pipe 15cm.

Raising the embankment is expensive but must be done if the run-out area is very flat and no place can be found where a deeper drain can discharge. If the bank is raised it must also be widened, so as to keep the 20 degree side slopes.

The second method is to lower the pipe. This means lowering the run-out drain 15cm and hence increasing its length, especially if the gradient of the ground is only slight. Soil from the nearer part of the run-out drain should be carried on to the embankment in a wheel-barrow. The upper drain (originally 45cm deep) could be deepened by 15cm too. Where there is a quick getaway for the water from the culvert pipe, i.e. a short run-out drain, this method of lowering the pipe is much cheaper than raising the embankment.

Obviously, in both cases a longer pipe will be necessary (because of the 20 degree slopes). Building a small wall of stones at each end will reduce the length of pipe required.

Notes on the Construction of Culverts
When laying the pipe make it straight so that sewer rods can, if necessary, be used to clean it out. Give it a crossfall of 8cm or more. The upstream end of the pipe should be cleared and a hole dug below the intake in case of silting. Subsequently, as a matter of routine, remove any debris near the entrance to the pipe.

Throwing Soil with Hoe or Shovel
If soil is to be shifted 6m or 8m by hand, as, for example, when making an embankment, do it as shown in Figure 63. Every portion of soil is thrown the full distance (A_1 to A_2: B_1 to B_2). If A_1 is thrown to B_2 time will be wasted double-handling it to A_2.

Excavation Below Embankment
A wide shallow drain may be dug along the lower side of an

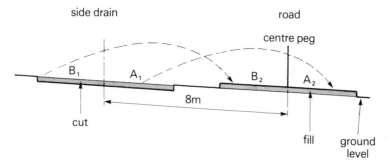

Figure 63. Throwing soil.

embankment (Figure 41) although it may not be necessary for purposes of drainage. It is done in order to provide soil for the downstream toe of the bank; the upper drain is too far away to do this.

Sinkage
A newly made embankment will always sink a little so allow at least 2cm extra for every 30cm of height when building it.

Design
Remember that a high embankment will be expensive. Design it no higher than necessary to provide adequate freeboard above the full supply level (f.s.l.) and adequate soil cover over the pipe.

Spring of Water under the Road
This forces water up from below, causing that part of the road to remain wet although the side drains on either side are efficient. An open drain should be dug to remove the spring water by gravity; the deeper the drain, the better. Enlarge the drain at the spring to make a wide hole. Lay sufficient length of cheap piping on the bed of the drain to take all the flow from the hole. Put big stones around the end of the pipe in the hole, with smaller stones above and smaller still on top. Finish off with soil for the road surface. If the pipe is deep enough and if the spring has all been opened up, a trickle of water will flow from the pipe and the whole road will dry satisfactorily.

PART 4

Maintenance

CHAPTER 10

Maintenance of Market Roads

The most important maintenance job is to see that every drain (lead-off, culvert, etc.) is functioning properly. This work is generally well suited to being carried out by hand. Further construction work may be necessary in order to improve the road, e.g. another lead-off drain or more cross-drainage may be required. If, at any time during the year, a weakness is noted which may cause, or has caused, some drain to stop functioning, the matter should be attended to without delay instead of leaving it until the annual maintenance.

1. Prevention of Flow Along the Carriageway

With time, wheel tracks will naturally tend to form on the carriageway as soil is pushed outwards to make a ridge. This is shown as ridge A in Figure 64. Another type of ridge (B in Figure 64) results from incorrect use of a road grader or from hoeing to clean the road surface by hand, the soil and rubbish being scraped outwards instead of inwards towards the centre. These ridges will prevent water being shed from the crown of the road into the side drains. Instead, it will flow along the road and by-pass the lead-off drains (Figure 65(a)).

The remedy for this situation is usually easy. Proceed as shown in

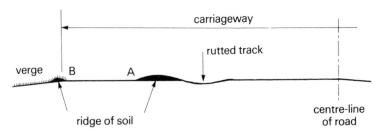

Figure 64. Formation of ridges in road surface.

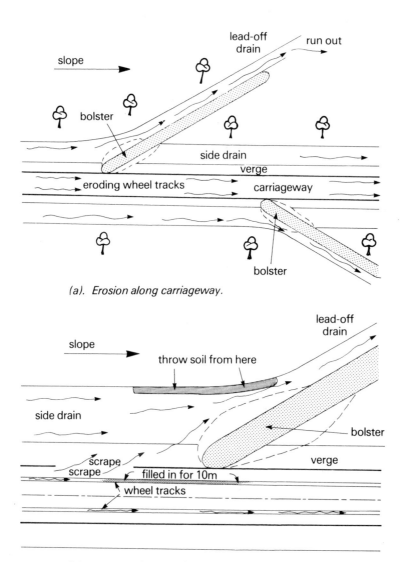

(a). Erosion along carriageway.

(b). Method of prevention.

Figure 65. Prevention of flow along carriageway.

Figure 65(b). A section of the eroded track is filled in by digging and throwing soil from the outer edge of the side drain and by cutting the corner of the lead-off drain. The ridge, or ridges, of soil must be cut down and spread, as indicated in Figure 65(b), so that the road surface resumes its original camber at that point and water is shed into the side drains. The result resembles a diversion bank that diverts the water out of an eroding footpath.

This work could be done at any point along the road but it is best to do it exactly in line with the lead-off bolster (Figure 65(b)). The latter is permanent and is easily seen so it will always be easy to find the exact section of track for filling-in in future years. As in the case of an ordinary diversion bank, the filled-in section of track, which is about 10m long, slopes both ways from the centre. Driving over it at speed, the bump is hardly noticeable but it is enough to divert all the flow out of the eroding track into the side drain. Water is not taken right across the road, as in the case of a village road diversion bank; instead, the flow from each track is diverted into the adjacent side drain. This filling-in operation, if it is done annually, ensures that each lead-off drain receives its fair share of water and that no storm water can pass on down the road to cause damage.

Periodic mechanical grading of the entire surface would be preferable but a grader may not be available. By restoring the camber on only a fraction of the length of the road, as described above, the cost is considerably reduced, without any reduction in erosion control.

2. Depth of Side Drains

It takes skill to set the levels of the side drains correctly, and in building the road errors may be made which should be corrected during maintenance. In Figure 37(b) the upper side drain is too shallow, giving insufficient camber on the road. This can be remedied by excavating the full width of the upper side drain slightly and throwing the soil onto the road. This will give a road of the correct profile, as in Figure 37(a). In Figure 37(c) the upper side drain has been dug too deep, so that the road is built up too much and there is danger of the side drain eroding. The drain can be filled up to the correct height by widening it slightly.

3. General Maintenance Operations

All water disposal and drainage problems must be dealt with first.

Afterwards, normal maintenance operations may be undertaken as detailed below.

Removing Tree Regrowth etc.
Dig out any leafy shoots, etc. by the roots so that they do not grow again. Big grass tussocks can also be dug out as they are a nuisance to traffic.

Repairing Pot-Holes
It is much cheaper to fill pot-holes with soil before or after the rains than to fill them with gravel during the rains. Nearly all places that give trouble due to mud formation can be put right, permanently, by constructing the correct earthworks so that all water drains away from the carriageway without delay.

Resurfacing the Road by Widening the Side Drains
Every year some soil is lost from the road surface in the form of dust in the dry season and mud in the rains. This loss must be replaced by throwing on more soil from the side drains. If this is not done the carriageway will get lower and lower and drainage will become more and more difficult in future years.

The soil is obtained by widening the side drains, digging and throwing the soil with a hoe or shovel on to the road. Dig down to the level of the bed of the side drain, leaving it flat and clean so that, when the grass grows, it will make an efficient grassed watercourse over the full width of the drain. If the drain is too narrow anywhere it must be widened. When the soil has to be dug for the road try to obtain it by widening the narrower places, if any, in the side drain. On the other hand, if more soil is not required urgently on the road do not waste time straightening an uneven outside edge of a side drain, if it is all wide enough already.

On crossfalls, only widen the upper side drain, not the lower.

Traffic Using Road During Resurfacing Operations
Do one half of the road first and allow traffic to use the other half. When all the new soil has been properly levelled on the first half, vehicles are allowed to run over it and the other half is then closed to traffic and resurfaced. Too much traffic must not be allowed to run on newly dug soil which has not been levelled.

Lead-Off Drains

If sand, etc. has been deposited in the lead-off drain remove it and dump it along the lower face of the lead-off bank or bolster. It is not suitable for putting on the road as it has no cohesion. Such water-borne deposits in the lead-off drain indicate erosion further up the slope. In many cases this can, and should, be put right.

Maintenance of Splashes

Filling in the ruts and potholes should be the only work necessary. To do this, bring in gravel or stones by lorry or by wheelbarrow. If any trees or shrubs are growing in the run-out they should be dug out and removed. If, instead, they are allowed to continue growing, the grass and sticks carried in the storm water will pile up against them and this may cause a blockage.

Road Work During Rains

Sometimes repairs, etc, have to be carried out on rainy days. Care must then be taken to avoid using soil that is too wet.

Consider a big hole being filled in a road which must continue to carry traffic. First all the water in the hole must be baled out. Finish with a small tin, and perhaps finally with a sack to soak up the final remains of moisture. Remove any wet mud. An hour or two of sunshine will help to dry the site. When filling, use only the driest soil that can be found, packing it down all the time. Leave it a little higher than the rest of the road so that it sheds the water.

If the mixture is dry enough there should be no future trouble but a small increase in moisture might well turn the whole mixture into a 'pudding' which would not dry out before the end of the rains and would cause perhaps month of trouble.

Similarly it is sometimes necessary to dig wet mud from the side drains for application to the road. In such cases heap the mud at the side of the road then spread it some weeks later when dry. Leave spaces between the heaps for the water to run off.

CHAPTER 11

Maintenance of Village Roads

1. Diversion Banks

Repair all diversion banks and insert new ones if it is considered necessary. Most existing diversion banks will need the addition of some soil to prevent them being easily broken. The crest of the bank must be maintained at its proper height, especially where the wheel tracks pass over it. If these tracks are not filled in, they may allow the water to pass over the top of the bank. Once a year, therefore, a skilled labourer should fill in any low places in the bank, as necessary. To get the required soil he cuts a little more off the inside of the curve of the drain, widening it slightly and improving the shape (Figure 44). The wider the drain, the safer it will be. Maintenance of diversion banks on paths follows exactly the same principles.

If he has a bicycle, one labourer can be made responsible for the maintenance of diversion banks on village roads throughout a wide area.

2. Clearing the Road

Remove all stumps and tree regrowth by digging deeply. Dig out stones or rock and break with a heavy hammer. Dig out tufts of grass. All long grass on the road could be cut, but generally this is not essential. If the grass is cut do not trouble to remove it but leave it where it is. It will do no harm on the road as long as graders are not used. Dry hay on a rural road does not inconvenience motor traffic or cyclists, so long as it does not conceal hidden stumps, etc. Growing anthills must be levelled and spread on the road. If necessary big ones can be poisoned with chemicals to prevent them growing again.

3. Filling in the Tracks

If labour is available, fill in the wheel tracks by digging soil from just outside the edge of the road, throwing into the track and spreading it (Figure 66(a)). Dig only on the upper side on crossfalls (Figure

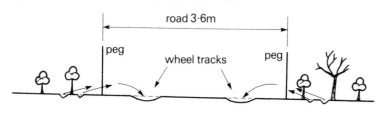

(a). No crossfall.

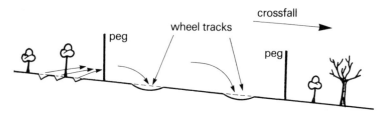

(b). With crossfall.

Figure 66. Filling in the tracks.

66(b)). Start filling in the tracks where the work is protected from erosion, i.e. just below a diversion bank or crest of a hill, then the new soil will not get washed away by a heavy storm.

4. Hoeing an Earth Road

Normally the road surface is not hoed at all but, if any hoeing is done, the soil must always be moved inwards towards the centre of the road. It is natural, perhaps, to want to scrape all rubbish, etc. off the road, dumping it in a line along the edge of the road, leaving the road clean. This policy should be avoided, since at each operation the surface of the road is lowered by a small amount because it is impossible to remove grass roots, etc. without removing topsoil as well.

The correct method is to scrape all rubbish, etc. from the outside towards the centre of the road and spread it there. If specially desired, the grass, etc. could be shaken out and carried off but this is generally a waste of time. Do not try to leave the road clean. To hoe the road correctly, therefore, the labourer must work facing outwards, towards the bush, with his back to the centre of the road.

5. Crossings

Wash-outs may have occurred where there is much cross drainage flowing over the road. These must be mended by filling in with soil and surfacing with gravel if necessary. It may be found that a low rock-filled gabion (see Chapter 9) is required in order to stabilise a difficult crossing.

CHAPTER 12

Rehabilitation of Roads

The situation sometimes arises where, rather than building a new road, it is necessary to rehabilitate an existing road to market or village road standard.

1. Market Roads

Removal of Storm Water
Whenever rehabilitating a stretch of old road, the first thing to do is to prevent any undue accumulation of storm water anywhere along the road, i.e. to remove it before it can do any serious damage.

The water must be forced off the road at suitable points. The necessary earthworks should be completed, if possible, before the rainy season begins, in order to avoid the expense of any further major erosion on the road. (This principle applies to village roads as well as to market roads.)

Where necessary, temporary diversion banks have to be constructed as an interim measure on market roads. The overseer must inspect the whole road and find all those points where the water can be made to flow away easily into the bush; always use a road tracer for this work.

Sites for splashes are obvious, but some of these may need diversion banks to make sure that no flood water can by-pass them. There will be other places where efficient diversion banks can be made at little cost. Some lead-off drains should also be feasible. If these diversion points are not too close together they should all be constructed and rendered storm-proof.

The overseer will then find that certain stretches of the road still remain unprotected and he must decide on the best way to protect them. Often temporary or permanent diversion banks provide the answer. Some of them may have to be large and expensive. Some lead-off drains may be made to work by raising the road in the vicinity of the lead-off bolster. These temporary diversion banks should be regarded as separate lengths of high-level road which have been completed earlier than the rest of the road. They force the water off the road in just the same way as a high-level road sheds water.

These banks will be very necessary on sunken roads on long gentle slopes for the first few years, until the crown of the road becomes well raised above average ground level. Make quite sure that the banks cannot break, especially those near the top of the hill.

The temporary diversion banks will no longer be required when the wide grassed side drains of this high-level market road have finally been completed.

Raising the Road

Suppose there is a rough narrow road 3m wide that has to be converted into a high-level market road. Consider Figure 67. The original road shown at ground level, is eroded in the tracks. The first year's work consists of widening each side by about 75cm making a 4.5m road, as shown. Stumps are dug out deeply; a gentle camber is made when levelling.

Similar operations annually will provide, in the fourth year, a well cambered road 9m wide including side drains (Figure 67). This is almost identical with the small high-level road made with the 2.1m stick.

Do not dig at all deeply the first year because any deep excavation that year would have to be filled in again by the subsequent

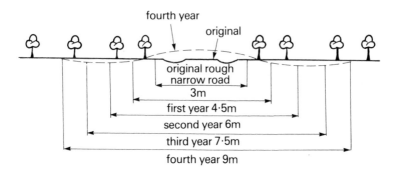

Figure 67. Raising the road.

operations. The widening is shown as being symmetrical but most, or all of it can, of course, be done on one side only. This will make it possible to cut corners so as to improve the road line.

This work could, of course, be completed in more or less than four years, according to requirements. Where there is continuity of policy and staff, there are definite advantages in doing a small amount each year. Better results can be obtained if the level of the road is raised to its full height in a series of separate operations. Stumping holes will be compacted by traffic, then filled up again when resurfacing is done and rolled in again. At the end of the four years there will be no holes at all and the whole surface will be equally hard. If, instead, the level is raised fully in one big digging operation the holes will become obvious as soon as traffic passes and they will continue to hold water indefinitely. With separate operations, improvements are made every time, e.g. cutting corners, adjusting slopes (filling in or cutting off) and so on.

The procedure of raising the road is the same whether erosion has occurred only in the wheel tracks (as in Figure 67), or across the whole carriageway.

In some cases deep gullies will have been eroded along the carriageway. There is no point in trying to mend these by filling them up with rock, stones or gravel; it might all get washed out. Even if it was successful and the gully mended, a new one would soon form alongside the old. The first thing to do is to remove all excess flow of water along the road; then the gully can be filled in with soil. This is much cheaper than the use of stone etc. All available stone should be preserved for building splashes, drifts, etc. where it is essential.

Relative Costs of Stumping a New Road Line Compared with Filling up an Eroded Road

The crown of a high-level road should be about 15cm above average ground level, irrespective of whether the road is new or whether it is a reconstructed road that was formerly sunken. In the latter case the side drains will be much larger than in the former, owing to the amount of extra fill required. This is expensive. The point is soon reached when it is cheaper to stump a new road line than to put an old sunken road in order.

Experience shows that, in lightly timbered country, it will be cheaper to stump a new road line if the old road has sunk more than

8cm below average ground level. In heavily timbered country a new road line should be considered when the old road has sunk more than 15cm.

Initial Work to be Undertaken on Inferior Roads
In the case of Figure 67 the first year's work is to widen the road by, say 1.5m. However, a lot of good can be done initially without widening the road at all, as shown in Figures 68(a) and (b).

Figure 68(a) shows some typical obstructions which may occur

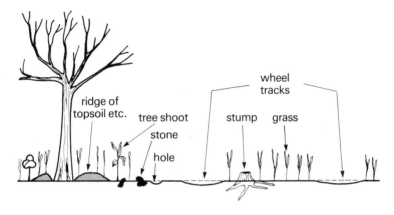

(a). Inferior road.

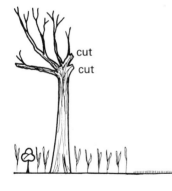

(b). Improved road.

Figure 68. Initial improvements.

along any road. All stumps must be dug out deeply; rocks must be removed or broken down with heavy hammers; the ridge of topsoil and rubbish at the edge must be returned to the road and everything must be levelled, leaving a slight camber and a reasonably straight road. Cut off any overhanging branches. All this will not cost much but it is a great improvement, as shown in Figure 68(b).

Reconstruction of Narrow Embankments
A low, narrow embankment will be expensive to reconstruct, as can be seen from Figure 69. To get the correct shape, big wide drains will have to be dug in order to fill in the old ones.

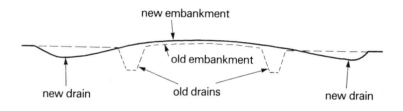

Figure 69. Reconstruction of narrow embankments.

Bank of Sand, etc. Along Edge of Side Drain
Where there is severe erosion and the run-off water carries a heavy load of silt, sand, etc. the latter tends to deposit in the side drain along the flatter stretches. Formerly, if the drain was not to silt up completely, the deposit had to be removed, by grader or by hand, and dumped in the bush alongside the drain. However, the most constructive thing to do first is to eliminate the source of the erosion so that silting ceases. Then dig and throw good soil from beyond the sandbank on to the road, in order to build it up.

Eroded Side Drains
Suppose the side drain of an old road has been badly eroded, as in Figure 70(a). The gully is easily mended by digging a new side drain in the correct position at the required height, so that enough soil is obtained to fill in the gully, and to raise the road if necessary. In this particular case, where the erosion is near the road, the side drain must be made to slope slightly outwards, as indicated in the dia-

gram, so that water does not tend to flow along the filled-in gully and erode the loose soil.

The new cross-section in Figure 70(a) has been made to resemble the standard high-level road made with the 2.1m stick, the only difference being that the side drain is a little deeper. The width, say 3m, is the same so it is wide enough.

In cases where further erosion is liable, the cut of the new side drain is only excavated about 1m wide to begin with and the road is raised. When the bed of this drain has grassed over, it can be widened again and the gully is then filled in level, as in Figure 70(a).

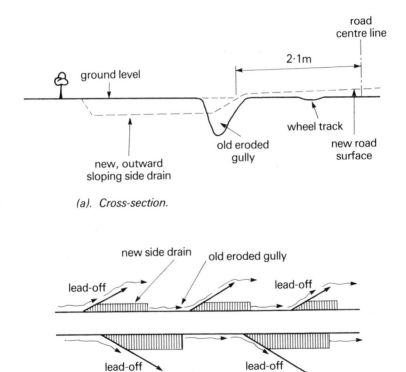

(a). Cross-section.

(b). Plan view.

Figure 70. Repair of eroded side drains.

Another safety measure is to complete the side drain as in Figure 70(a), tackling only the top half of each interval between lead-off drains Figure 70(b). This portion of the side drain is well protected by the lead-off drain above it and it will therefore be less liable to erode than the lower half. After a rainy season, when the upper half has grassed over well, the lower half can be tackled.

2. Village Roads

Adjust the line where necessary, then site the diversion banks. This must be done with care because on these village roads the banks will be permanent.

In the case of an eroded, sunken road, when all the diversion banks have been constructed, filling in of the road itself can be commenced starting immediately below each diversion bank (Figure 70(b) illustrates a somewhat similar principle). If the road is filled in up to former ground level then water will be able to flow across it at any point instead of flowing along the road until it reaches the next diversion bank.

If funds are very short, the following system may be allowed so long as all diversion banks are kept fully stormproof.

Take the case where the old road has become badly gullied, due to the force of water flowing along it; if efficient diversion banks are constructed this flow of water will cease. It will then soon be found that the gullies, potholes, etc. begin to silt up, especially when the grass growth begins to protect them. There will thus be a gradual improvement in the running surface of the road without any attention being paid to the surface at all. This emphasises the need to establish diversion banks throughout a village road system at the earliest possible date if reconstruction is to be undertaken.

APPENDIX 1

Surveying Techniques and Equipment

1. Gradients

When explaining work on earth roads it is necessary to describe the various gradients or slopes required. Figure A1 shows how this is done.

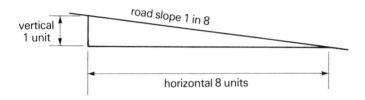

Figure A1. Gradient.

A slope is expressed as the amount of vertical rise over a given horizontal distance, both distances being expressed in the same units. Figure A1 shows a road that rises 1cm vertical for every 8cm horizontal. This is the same slope as one rising 1m vertical for every 8m horizontal, or 1mm vertical in 8mm horizontal and so on. They all give the same slope of 1 unit in 8 units which is a slope of 1 in 8.

In some countries gradients are expressed in percentages. Thus a 2% slope means 2 in 100 which is 1 in 50; a 10% slope is 10 in 100 or 1 in 10; and so on. In this book, gradients are always expressed as '1 in . . .'

2. Pacing

If rural road work is to be done efficiently, both the overseer and the foreman should be able to measure the distances quickly and accurately by pacing. This might be required when surveying, measuring gradients, giving out tasks, measuring the width of village roads, and so on.

To check one's pacing proceed as follows: insert two pegs exactly

30m apart and pace between them a few times, adjusting the length of pace so that it takes exactly 30 even paces to cover the distance. Each pace will then be 1m long. If you take 29 paces to cover the 30m distance you are pacing too strongly; if you take 31 paces you are not strong enough. Always measure to the ball of the foot, not to the heel nor to the toe.

Such pegs should be fixed at every field station, office, or temporary construction camp. Check your pacing every day before starting work and again after finishing, when you are tired, so that you can always pace accurately.

3. Road Tracers

A road tracer consists essentially of a hollow pipe with a very small hole in the middle of one end and an opening with a horizontal mark in the middle of the other end. Its own weight makes it hang horizontally (Figure A2).

The instrument swings from a peg or nail fixed near the top of a wooden staff about 1.8m high (Figure A4). The road tracer itself is about 30cm high so the tube is about 1.5m from the ground, roughly at eye level. Most instruments are usually adjusted, when necessary, by shifting the tube but it is really better if the tube is welded to the frame so that it cannot shift and adjustments are made, instead, by shifting a weighted metal clip (Figure A2) which can be moved along the tube either way, as required, and then tightened.

The target (Figure A3) consists of a stick nearly 2m long with a crossbar on it, the centre of which is exactly the same height above ground as the centre of the road tracer tube on the staff. The top half of the target is painted white. The exact height of the tube is first marked on the crossbar and a scale in cm is marked above and below from this point.

When looking through the tube of the road tracer, which is at position A in Figure A4, it is seen to 'hit' the target (at position B) at, say, the 16cm mark *above* the crossbar on the scale. Ground level at B is therefore 16cm *lower* than ground level at A. If these two points are 20m apart it means that there is a fall from A to B of 1 in 125 if the slope between these two points is uniform; this slope is indicated in the diagram (not to scale).

The road tracer is read by the overseer or by the foreman and a labourer holds the target. When reading the road tracer it is best to say, 'You are (or he is) 12cm down' (or whatever the reading is)

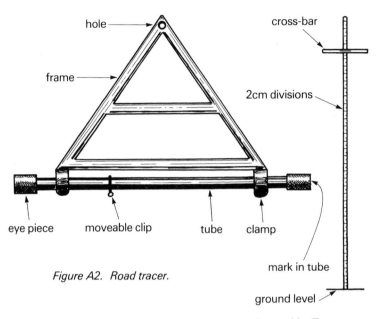

Figure A2. *Road tracer.*

Figure A3. *Target.*

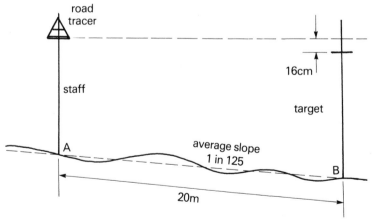

Figure A4. *Use of road tracer and target.*

rather than 'I am 12cm up'. Always say whether the target is up or down, then call (or signal) to the labourer to move uphill or downhill as the case may be, in order to find the required position for the correct gradient. The position of B in Figure A4 would be correct for a lead-off drain flowing from A to B. As with any levelling instrument care must be taken not to read a rise for a fall, and vice versa.

Remember that, when pegging a gradient, it is the distances between the final pegs that count. In other words, if a fall of, say, 1 in 100 is being pegged, there will be a drop of 6cm every 6m or 12cm every 12m and so on. If the labourer with the target is 6m from the road tracer the fall at that point may show, say, 2cm instead of 6cm. The target must then be moved down the hill (4cm vertical) to give the required 6cm fall but the distance measured from the road tracer (6m) must remain the same. The target labourer must therefore learn to walk along the circumference of a circle, the radius being, in this case, 6m. In other words he must move round as if he is holding the end of a string 6m long with the other end fixed to the road tracer.

Remember also that a road tracer can never be a very accurate instrument. A careful reading taken at a distance of 10m may be 2cm wrong, due perhaps to the effect of wind on the road tracer.

Suppose a road tracer shows that a drain slopes downhill 1cm in 10m from X to Y, that is, a slope of 1 in 1000: if it is correct, water will flow down this gentle slope from X to Y. If, however, this reading on the target at Y happened to be 2cm too low, the true reading would be 2cm higher and so would show a *rise* of 1cm in 10m from X to Y, i.e. a rise of 1 in 1000. The water would therefore, in fact, flow gently from Y to X and *not*, as originally thought, from X to Y. A mistake like this could have serious consequences.

This example shows that a road tracer is unreliable for measuring gradients flatter than about 1 in 300; it is a most useful instrument, however, for measuring steeper gradients such as are required in road work. Consider, for example, a lead-off drain pegged with a road tracer at a gradient of 1 in 100 (6cm in 6m). If this reading is 2cm out either way, the gradient could become 6−2=4cm in 6m, which is 1 in 150, or it could become 6+2=8cm in 6m, or 1 in 75. Both 1 in 75 and 1 in 150 would work all right on a lead-off drain so no difficulty arises.

When taking readings with the road tracer it should be swung slightly before each reading and three or four independent readings should be made at each point instead of only one, just to make sure the right answer is obtained.

If the overseer only has his horizontally adjusted road tracer to use in hilly country he can, of course, calculate any gradient by measuring the distance and then measuring the difference in height on the road tracer. Thus if he wishes to find an upward slope of 1 in 10 for his road line across a hill, he will need to find a point which is 50cm higher (a rise of 50cm) in 5m. If the target labourer paces 10m the difference on the road tracer must show 1m. At 15m he would need a reading of 1.5m below the crossbar (i.e. near the foot of the target) if the gradient is to be 1 in 10.

Always read *up* the hill if the vertical interval is more than a few centimetres, otherwise the cross mark will be off the target.

4. Dumpy and Surveyor's Levels

In very flat country a more accurate instrument than a road tracer, such as a Dumpy level or a Surveyor's level, may be required. In some places this might show that a different layout would be preferable. In such cases it would be worthwhile getting the job done with the more accurate instrument.

During the rains any long stretches of standing water will, of course, show exactly which way the slope runs, without the help of any instruments at all. A wide side drain full of water would defintely flow if the slope is as little as 1 in 5000 especially if there is no grass growth to impede the movement of water. The overseer does not necessarily have to know exactly how much the gradient is but he does have to know for certain which way the water is going to flow when the road is made.

In the hands of a competent foreman a road tracer is perfectly adequate for nearly all road work: a more delicate, expensive instrument would have definite disadvantages.

5. Checking and Adjusting the Road Tracer

Overseers and foremen must be able to check their road tracers themselves.

To do this, first hold the target alongside the road tracer on a level floor and make a pencil mark at the exact spot on the crossbar where the road tracer points when it is swinging freely; this should be in the centre of the crossbar. Place the road tracer on the ground at a point

A and select a point B about 20m distant that shows exactly level with A. Then move the road tracer to point B and put the target on point A (i.e. swop around). If the road tracer is correctly adjusted it will, of course, show level in that position, i.e. it will 'hit' the target at A exactly on the pencil mark in the middle of the crossbar.

This should be done every morning and whenever there is the slightest reason to suspect that the adjustment may have altered. There is no excuse for anyone using a road tracer which is out of adjustment.

Suppose the back sight from B to A 'hits' the target at A, say 8cm below the mark on the crossbar, as in Figure A5. This shows that the road tracer requires adjustment. To do this, adjust the road tracer to indicate a point which is *half the error*; in other words, in this case, the error being 8cm below, the road tracer must be made to point 4cm below the crossbar. It will then be reading horizontal. Finally, check normally, to ensure there has been no mistake.

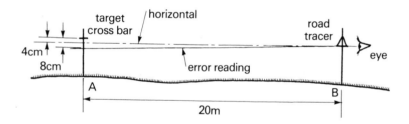

Figure A5. Checking and adjusting the road tracer.

6. Checking and Adjusting the Surveyor's Level
The principle is exactly the same as that for the road tracer but sights of 0.5 to 1km are taken instead of only 20m.

7. Boning Rods
A set of boning rods consists simply of three straight sticks about 1.3m long, all exactly the same length. Having fixed a rod vertically on a height peg (see section 9, below) at either end of the area in question (e.g. the place where a long gabion is to be constructed) the third rod is also held vertical and is moved along the line between the two fixed rods, as indicated in Figure A6. By sighting along the tops of the rods any point on the line can be marked.

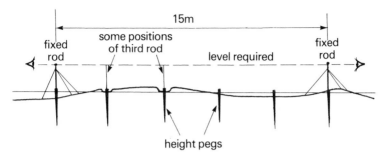

Figure A6. Use of boning rods.

If required, this method can be used on gradients, e.g. to check the excavation of a run-out drain. All that is required is the correct height mark at either end of the stretch to be checked.

Every foreman on rural road work should cut threee boning rods and keep them for use when required. Boning rods will not be necessary when the eye can easily see the line of the tops of all the height pegs, but this is not feasible in a situation like that in Figure A6. If all height pegs show some distance above ground level (Figure 60(b) and Figure 47 before filling in), sighting can be done easily by eye without using boning rods.

8. Survey Pegs

Survey pegs are strong, straight sticks used to mark the dimensions of an earthwork. They should be well hammered in as they may have to stay in position for many months. In the case of an embankment their tops are also levelled to show the final soil level. An example of their use is given in Chapter 9, Section 3.

9. Height Pegs

A peg is often needed that will indicate the required soil level at a glance; it must therefore stand up slightly above the final soil level so that it can be seen readily from some distance away, and will not be covered when the earthwork is complete. This is called a height peg (Figure A6). These height pegs are inserted at intervals, along the edge of the earthwork, the top of each peg being carefully levelled. The soil at the peg is raised or lowered so that all pegs show exactly the same amount; it may be 2cm or more, as preferred. An

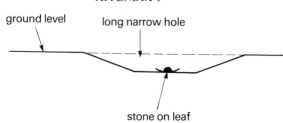

Figure A7. Preserving marks below ground level.

example of their use is given in Chapter 9, Section 3. This method is accurate and easy to understand.

10. Preserving Marks Below Ground Level

When surveying it is often necessary to preserve marks made below ground level. The best way to do this is to dig a long narrow hole sloping down to the required depth (Figure A7). Make a long, flat, firm bed at exactly the correct height then lay a large leaf on it and put a stone on top to keep it in place. To take subsequent readings remove the leaf and replace afterwards. This method is quicker than inserting height pegs in the holes (showing 2cm above the level mark). It may also be used for making marks on, and above, the surface.

APPENDIX 2
Glossary

Bank Diversion A bank in a market road designed to ensure removal of all flow in the event of a culvert or splash becoming blocked. Not quite the same as a diversion bank.

Bolster The earth bank at the mouth of a lead-off drain; it blocks the side drain, thus diverting all running water into the lead-off drain.

Boning Rods See Appendix 1.

Camber A cambered road is one which is raised in the middle so that it sheds water equally into either side drain.

Carriageway The central portion of the road, 3.6m wide, where vehicles run. On a cambered road this is 1.8m either side of the centre line.

Catchwater Drain A narrow channel designed to prevent surface run-off water from reaching the road.

Compaction, Consolidation Making soil hard by rolling, tamping, etc. or by the passage of traffic.

Cross-drainage Water flowing, either over the road, as at a drift or a splash or a diversion bank, or under the road, as at a bridge or through a culvert or a small pipe.

Crossfall When a road runs at an angle across a slope there is a crossfall; when it runs straight down the slope or along the flat there is no crossfall.

Cross-section Imaginary view of something, as if it were cut through.

Crown of Road The highest point of a cambered carriageway when seen in cross-section; it is normally the centre of the road.

Cut Dig out, excavate soil; opposite to 'fill'.

Direction bank A low bank which controls the direction of water flow at any point off the road.

Diversion bank A long low bank on a village road, designed to remove all flow of water from the road.

Diversion drain The drain of a diversion bank.

Drainage, road drainage   The control and disposal of surface run-off water.

Drift   A stream or river crossing where the water flows over the road; it is bigger than a splash.

Erosion   The removal of soil by running water.

Fill   Fill in, build up; opposite to 'cut'.

Flat country   Country which appears flat to the eye; this may include slight undulations with a slope of 1 in 100 or gentler.

Flood, flood water   Excessive flow in a stream or drain.

Foreman   The man in charge of a gang of road labourers. He takes instructions from the overseer.

Freeboard   Height above standing water.

f.s.l. (full supply level)   The level of the water when it is just flowing.

Gabion   Loose stones held in place by wire netting, the edges of which are tied together.

Gradient   A slope; see Appendix 1.

Gravel   Coarse sand and small stones; in this book it refers to any natural material like gravel which is transported on to the road from a distance in order to improve the running surface of the road.

Hump   A gentle bump, e.g. above a culvert.

Lead-off, lead-off drain   A drain that leads water from the side drain into the bush.

Market Road   A road designed to carry up to about 50 vehicles per day.

Km/h   Kilometres per hour.

Overseer   The officer in charge of the work in the district; he is responsible for the work of the foreman.

Road, roadway   Used here to denote the carriageway and verges, i.e. the area lying between the side drains, if any are present.

Road material   The soil etc. with which the road is built up.

Run-out   Where a drain discharges water into the bush.

Saddle   A low point on a watershed line.

Scour, scouring action   Erosion of an earth surface by water running too fast.

Side drain   The drain excavated along one, or both, sides of a market road, the soil from which goes to raise the level of the road.

Silt   Sand and soil carried away by fast-moving water but deposited by slow-moving or stationary water.

Sinkage   Subsidence of road surface due to compaction (consolidation).

Splash   Where road drainage water flows across the surface of the road. It may, or may not, be in a natural watercourse, and is smaller than a drift.

Storm   Refers here to very heavy rain and not to wind, etc.

Task, task work   A set amount of work.

Wheel tracks   The two marks, about 1.8m apart, made by a four-wheeled vehicle always running in the same position. Eventually they will become two deep ruts.

Verge   The area of the road between the edge of the carriageway and the side drain.

Village road   A road designed to carry a few vehicles per day.

Watercourse   A natural drainage channel, which may sometimes be dry.

Watershed   The line of high land which water flows away from on both sides.

Waterway   Used here for an artificial watercourse designed to convey water; a grassed channel.